THE DOWBEATERS
How to Buy Stocks That Go Up

THE DOWBEATERS
How to Buy Stocks That Go Up

New Revised Edition

by Ira U. Cobleigh and Bruce K. Dorfman

Macmillan Publishing Company
New York

Collier Macmillan Publishers
London

Macmillan Publishing Company
866 Third Avenue, New York, N.Y. 10022
Collier Macmillan Canada, Inc.

Library of Congress Cataloging in Publication Data

Cobleigh, Ira U.
    The Dowbeaters : how to buy stocks that go up.

    Bibliography: p.
    Includes index.
    1. Investments—United States—Handbooks, manuals, etc. 2. Stocks—United States—Handbooks, manuals, etc. I. Dorfman, Bruce K. II. Title.
HG4921.C595   1984   332.63′22   84-11288
ISBN 0-02-526490-7

Macmillan books are available at special discounts for bulk purchases for sales promotions, premiums, fund-raising, or educational use. Special editions or book excerpts can also be created to specification. For details, contact:

Special Sales Director
Macmillan Publishing Company
866 Third Avenue
New York, New York 10022

10 9 8 7 6 5 4 3 2 1

Printed in the United States of America

Dedicated to
Truth, Justice, and the
American Way . . .

Contents

PART THREE

DOWBEATER INVESTMENTS

PART FOUR

DOWBEATER SPECULATIONS

Introduction

Dear Dowbeater,

Here is the hottest new edition of our foresighted book, *The Dowbeaters*, which identified exciting opportunities for gainful investment in the stock market. At the time of our first Dowbeater adventure, the Dow Jones Industrial Average was in the 800 range; and dozens of excellent common stocks were selling at low multiples and well below book value. Many of those selections exploded in the years since. Our recommendations on silver were particularly timely because in 1979 Hecla Mining was the largest gainer on the NYSE, increasing during the year from low to high by over 900 percent as the price of silver rose 1000 percent within fourteen months of publication. Our average silver stock gained 222 percent from November 1978 to April 1981.

Dowbeater bank stock increased 49 percent during the same period. Takeover stocks jumped 128 percent. Lazarus stocks scored an average gain of 107 percent. Corporate bonds increased 3 percent and convertible bonds increased 18 percent.

The Herzfeld Hedge identified dozens of funds that increased 20 percent or more, and the switching of the Eclipse Method of Investing identified the major stock-market turning points. It spotlighted the ideal times for buying and selling America's leading mutual funds, creating gains of 50 percent to 100 percent on major mutual funds.

These results confirm our opinion that if one is properly informed, and follows the guidelines of fundamental and technical analysis, it is possible for the nonprofessional investor to identify and select undervalued securities that within fifteen months can outperform the Dow Jones Average.

Not only is it possible to winnow winners from the forty thousand different issues of common stocks quoted or traded with some frequency each week, but the attention and research you devote to enhancing the value of your portfolio can add excitement to your life! If you are evaluating and following the market action of a list of securities on a regular basis, you should never be bored. Each day ushers in a new set of market conditions, and as the year 2000 approaches, we believe Wall Street will surge in speculative action not witnessed in generations.

You can be a part of this wave on Wall Street, and *The Dowbeaters* can help you share in America's future prosperity.

IRA U. COBLEIGH
BRUCE K. DORFMAN
March 1984

PART ONE
DOWBEATER
TIMING

▯

America at
Book Value!

Are you prepared for the coming explosive stock-market boom?

The Dowbeaters represents a milestone in investment conceptualization. It heralds one of the greatest investment opportunities in over a generation.

Do you have an investment plan?

This book is as pragmatic as it is profound. *The Dowbeaters*, utilizing the world-renowned Dow Jones Industrial Average to measure the pulse of the American economy, takes an evolutionary leap from present-day investment philosophies. No one method, technique, stock, or stock group is absolute. *The Dowbeaters* builds multilevel investment strategies for those who can seize the opportunity of a unique investment juncture for America. This is a time that affords investors maximum opportunity with minimal risks—a time that finds the subtle positive winds of economic change unnoticed by panic-stricken investors.

This exciting Wall Street adventure into economic time will show you how to invest when most are apathetic and pessimistic, extrapolating our present economic plight into oblivion. The book utilizes the strengths of tested investment-management techniques and timing methods for those investors seeking to compound their investment capital in the coming decade.

The Dowbeaters is multidimensional; it draws upon the great fundamental and technical research available today. It is the synthesis of decades of research in actual application by Wall Street professionals. It is a book that is purposely being released at a unique time for investors.

Are you interested in fast speculative gain?

The Dowbeaters presents a broad spectrum of investment techniques. Not only will this book show you how to compound and build investment capital throughout bull and bear markets, but it also identifies the scores of stocks we feel are most likely to outperform the Dow Averages during the market's forthcoming price explosion. And for speculators with the patience and courage to participate in low-priced stock speculation, we select specific mini-stocks.

Do you know how the economic forces of supply and demand are operating to create the coming price explosion in the Dow Averages?

The Dowbeaters identifies the catalysts for the coming bull market which will explode prices to new all-time highs.

The catalysts are masked in today's negative investment environment, but are about to launch the Dow Averages into headline news, day after day, as record millions join the rush to own common stocks.

Are you concerned about the potential risks in investing?

You will find out how the rich get richer. This plan is ideal for the coming decade and can give you the peace of mind necessary to any successful investment program.

Do you want to eliminate guesswork from investing?

This book goes right to the core of investing psychology. We show the fundamental investment parameters that have existed throughout this century. *The Dowbeaters* shows the continual value relationships that motivate stock prices, and how to identify strategic times to invest for low-risk, high-gain returns.

The Dowbeaters is more than an investment guide. It will show you the counterbalancing forces that are acting to undermine the economic negatives of today's economic stagnation. You will have a roadmap for the future to help you anticipate, instead of react. This book will help you score significant gains on Wall Street and improve your net worth. This book will show you how to buy stocks that go up!

America at Book Value!

America, as revealed through the message of the Dow Jones Industrial Average, is for sale near book value. At only a few times in Dow history has America sold below book value. Each time has flashed a remarkable investment opportunity —a golden opportunity for investors to have their cake and eat it too! This is an opportunity to buy and hold; to receive both dividends and long-term capital gains; to build fortunes in low-priced stocks. When investors buy near book value, they are buying today's assets and not tomorrow's promises. They are not speculating on the unknown.

Here are the few select times when the Dow has sold below book value in the past fifty years:

July 1932	Dow 41.22	The low point of the Depression and the low year of the century for the Dow Averages.
April 1942	Dow 92.92	World War II had undermined the future security of the United States.
June 1949	Dow 160.62	Postwar recessionary fears were being extrapolated into a Depression.
December 1974	Dow 577.60	Watergate had created a credibility crisis for the dollar. Depression thought imminent.
October 1978	Dow 789.67	Monetary crisis heats up, creating fear of all paper mediums. The dollar at all-time lows against many major currencies.
November 1983	Dow 1287.20	All-time high.

Now, after inflation, recession, and languid public pessimism, stocks are being moved into the hands of the "few." These financial elite, and Arab and European investors, are gobbling up the stock certificates of American corporations and locking them away in their bank vaults. This is happening now while the light of reason is concealed from most investors by dark, overhanging economic clouds. These clouds obscure the true economic picture and the potentials for the dawn of an economic explosion on a grand scale.

As day follows night, the crowd's languid economic mood is certain to end, as does every economic phase. By reflection and insight, which you will gain from reading this book, you can separate yourself from current negative thinking.

Panic waves of fear and uncertainty, occurring with cyclical regularity, have repeatedly driven the prices of stocks down to rewarding buying levels throughout history. Few realize that the major economic problems of today are difficult more because of our subjectivity than their reality. For example, our recent economic problem, inflation, reached comparable intensity both in 1921 and 1949.

The problems that we solved in the post–World War II era were actually not very different from the ones that plague us today. Then, as now, postwar inflation was linked with a stale, stagnant economy. (From a historical perspective, inflations have frequently preceded booms and *not* led to the political and social unrest that is currently thought likely. What we are plagued with—what dominates our economy and the whole system of capitalism—is a major lack of faith in man for his fellow man and in the basic paper mediums used to conduct business.) Recently, due to inflation fears, the dollar, stocks, and bonds were being dumped at historically low levels of valuation. Many market observers had become so gloomy that they predicted a complete breakdown of our economic system. But what investors don't realize is that right now, major positive forces are emerging as a result of the dramatic shifts in valuations of the dollar on the world currency market.

As these signs become readily apparent, the grand bull

market will be unfolding. Since 1966, the Dow Jones has made meager progress on the upside. It seems now, though, that the bear market is over. Soon we will find that the dollar will be low enough to ignite an explosive boom, beginning a major bull market. This will start the grand economic upmove.

The Dowbeaters is based on the belief that with a new economic ground swell, the methods and companies identified in this book will ride the crest of this wave into the new decade. Lightning is about to strike!

The book value, earnings, and dividends of the Dow Averages have doubled since 1964, but the Dow quotations have not advanced to mirror these higher values. During the last decade, each and every year until 1983 has found the Dow in the 800–900 zone at some time. Since this same period has contained such a massive fundamental growth leap in dividends and earnings, we feel that the Dow is now at bedrock levels.

Along with this internal fundamental growth, we have also witnessed a soaring gross national product. This has occurred in spite of five presidents in sixteen years, a war, an inflation, and mass public pessimism. One set of negatives after another, yet the Dow is at the same levels and is fundamentally stronger than ever!

This is therefore a confident book designed to dispel gloom and to view in the distance the return of a vibrant capitalistic economy, affording once again fortune-building opportunities in the stock market such as existed in such profusion in the post–World War II boom.

We predict a renaissance of exuberance in the stock market—a renewed zeal for speculation in the 1980s and beyond. America will overcome its inertia, bounce back, and resume its earlier pre-eminence in productive efficiency and its traditional leadership in technological breakthroughs.

We predict a bull market of the grandest proportions, which will move the Dow Average to 2000 or higher! Here we explain how you can profit from this new investment climate, and outline the rules for accumulating an appropriate portfolio of stocks. The strategies given in this book will cover the investment spectrum from conservative to very speculative.

This book differs from most on securities and investment because it uses the Dow Jones Industrial Average alone as its constant point of reference. We suggest a continuing comparison between the market performance of individual stocks and/or a portfolio and the performance of the DJIA. To be a "Dowbeater," a stock, researched to blend income with capital gain, must consistently outpace "the Dow." If in addition the stock should double or triple in price, is split, or increases its dividend—then so much the better!

It is our sincere belief that it is possible to identify superior action stocks through incisive research and using the following time-tested criteria. Such stocks should, in general:

1. be in uptick or "turnaround" industries;
2. evidence rising earning power;
3. have a positive technical chart;
4. sell below the prevailing DJIA multiple;
5. trade in active volume;
6. be low-priced, preferably below $20, for animate market motion;
7. have some special attraction likely to stimulate market interest;
8. have an energetic, innovative, and stock-owning management;

9. in certain cases, be an acquisition candidate;
10. earn 12 percent or more on stockholder's equity;
11. document a growth rate of 12 percent or more annually; and
12. relate to a young company with unusual products and a small capitalization.

Investments with most of these characteristics have usually performed well in the past and appear likely to continue doing so in the future.

We stress the importance of low multiples because of the costly mistakes made by even sophisticated investors (individual as well as institutional) who in 1968–72 found themselves paying forty to sixty times earnings for glamour stocks—to their great sorrow.

Thus, in recent years, there have been myriads of investors whose results in Wall Street have proved disappointing. In 1968 there were approximately 30 million common stockholders in America. Today there are 42 million. There are myriads more who would like to enter the market now (and, incidentally, expand the reservoir of equity capital in Ameriica) should they encounter a dependable method for screening securities.

There are basically four separate investment philosophies we recommend, any one of which, intelligently pursued, should prove rewarding over time: the Lowry Eclipse Method, the Herzfeld Hedge, the Dowbeater Stocks and Bonds, and the Dowbeater Speculations. You will find each method unique and capable of standing on its own strengths —you can select the one that appeals most to your investment philosophy. You will also find that you can combine methods to customize a strategy that will attain the long-term financial rewards possible in the 1980s.

Now the press, radio, and television again exude bullishness. A mood of optimism is surfacing as the DJIA heads toward new all-time highs. The stock market again will be center stage as a topic of conversation; the speculative languor of the past few years will fade away. New stories of corporate gain and glamour will be bruited about; new stocks, tips, and rumors will animate and motivate market action.

"Looks like the small investor is finally getting back into the market." (*Drawing by Chas. Addams;* © 1976 *The New Yorker Magazine, Inc.*)

Wall Street will hum, as the crowd reverses its viewpoint and new investors awake to the coming era. Enter the brave bulls, with herds of sheep following them. For most investors, the roar of the crowd and the trading volume that accompanies high prices are just what is needed for them to join the rush. But the greatest success will come only to those few who can apply logic and patience to investment decisions and who act in the vanguard of the economy's next move. Wake up, America!

2

The Grand American
Economic Supercycle

History shows us that our nation's economy has operated on a grand supercycle throughout this century. This supercycle, which seems to span several decades, has four phases. The first phase is war: During wartime, the nation's efforts are directed toward defense and armaments, providing the foodstuffs and equipment that a war demands of the economy.

The second phase of the cycle is usually a price inflation. Many of the goods produced in wartime are economic dead ends—the country has invested its time and money in products that are not reusable in the economy. After the war ends, there naturally arises a massive demand for civilian goods. The resulting postwar inflation may run for three to five years, reaching levels of inflation in the region of 5 to 6 percent, with bulges up to 14 percent or higher.

It is during this three-to-five-year period after a war that the judgment on runaway inflation should be made. If inflation does not reach double-digit proportions for longer than two consecutive years, the problems of runaway inflation should not be overemphasized. What happens instead is stage three, during which the currency of the country is brought down to a low enough level on the world markets to finance and stimulate an export boom. This export boom will usually carry the country into a major industrial supercycle upmove. During this stage, foreign countries buy the goods and services of the country and also invest heavily in its growth.

This phase-three boom eventually reaches runaway proportions; it carries within it the seeds of its own destruction. After this, the fourth stage ushers in either depression or severe recession. During this period, the overextension of credit and excesses of the boom are atoned for. It is during this period that paper money and bloated credits used for business reach levels greatly extended in terms of real long-term value, and depression or severe recession are the correctives. Usually this stage planes down all the crests of stage three, which was the runaway upmove of the supercycle, and brings us back down to the beginning of another cycle.

This grand supercycle has existed throughout this century in the economic history of our country, and of the Dow Averages. Stage one was World War I. This period lasted for about two years; following it, three years later in 1921, we had an inflation of very severe proportions. This raised the cost of commodities to extremely high levels and brought down the value of the U.S. dollar on the world markets, which was stage two. Following the inflation of 1921, we entered stage three—the Dow Jones Averages and the industrial boom soared to giddy new highs. The Dow Averages rose from a level of 100 up to 380 in eight years. This era highlighted the extension of credit, the return of credibility of the dollar, and the return of confidence in the financial instruments of business. Faith returned to such an extent that we had a massive new-issue boom near the top (1928–29) and entry of the public in droves into the stock market.

Stage three ended with the swollen climax in the market and a collapse into the Great Depression from 1929 until 1932. This dismal depression was the herald for stage four, which exorcised the excesses of stage three and realigned the value of securities, commodities, and real estate at distressingly low prices.

The 1929 crash sent shock waves rippling through the stock market for decades afterward. With the crash over, the Dow Averages moved up with vigor from 1932 to 1937, as a modicum of confidence was restored. This market uptrend developed, ironically, during the worst period of the Depression—a classic case of the market moving ahead of the economy. This is because the stock market is more of a barometer than a thermometer. Thermometers record, but barometers project or foretell, and that is why the Dow has in most instances discounted the import of business news (by the time such news becomes public knowledge).

The easy-credit environment of the 1920s was over. Stocks could no longer be purchased on margin of only 10 percent. Business was conducted on such old-fashioned concepts as credit worthiness. Orders were paid for in advance, and bankers looked for collateral. Money was scarce. The volume during this period was created by fewer investors, those in sound financial condition, who sought seasoned stocks where the yields were high. Trading volume, even though the prices of the averages were half what they had been ten years previous, was sharply diminished, so that the value of transactions in this postcrash era fell. Investors generally were using assets salvaged from the erosion of depression, and only slowly rebuilding their resources for equity investment.

From 1932 until the early 1940s, stocks flowed back into the hands of wealthy long-term investors; it was a classic opportunity for buying stocks for pure investment value. The market was returning to undervaluation after an excessive speculative splurge. Shares in many companies were selling at book value or less. The dismal economic news, extensive press coverage of high unemployment, slow recovery, and impending war, had moved stocks out of the hands of weak, undercapitalized individuals into the hands of the wealthy investors resourceful enough to withstand adverse interim price swings and retain their positions for long-term investment growth on a grand scale.

The resurgent years of 1932 to 1942 found steep, precipitous breaks in the market followed by rallies and then again steep breaks. But the breaks during this period failed to penetrate the 1932 lows. In fact, the whole period was a slow assimilation of the excess supplies of stock—a period of base-building and reassessment of the country's potential future. The years following proved the 1932–42 phase to be a time of major opportunity; it is very important to realize that this period found the country in one of its most negative moods.

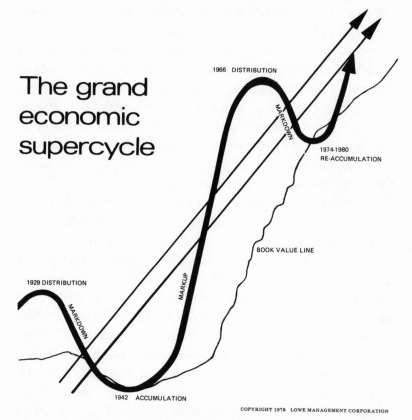

The grand economic supercycle

1966 DISTRIBUTION

MARKDOWN

1974-1980
RE-ACCUMULATION

BOOK VALUE LINE

1929 DISTRIBUTION

MARKUP

MARKDOWN

1942 ACCUMULATION

Chart 1 The Grand Economic Supercycle: This four-stage rhythmic pattern begins when the Dow Averages are below book value. As can be seen from the chart, we are now bottoming and accelerating to the upside.

The Cycle Repeats

With World War II, we again entered stage one of the grand economic supercycle. The industrial strength of this country was restored to normal levels, but the cost of war induced inflation. In the early 1950s, inflation again occurred three to five years after a war, and reached very high levels.

Stock prices were still low, especially compared with a decade later. With the Korean War past, the market began climbing at a steeper pace, generating one wave after another, bringing the Dow to new heights. This grand bull market was on its way to a new series of high plateaus. Every reaction witnessed in 1953 and 1957 and in 1962 was followed by a new all-time high. Stocks were snapped up as confident investors flocked back into the market.

Speculation was becoming more and more in vogue, and investing for dividend return was no longer the prime motivation. Investors sought the quick, exciting gains that come from fast upmovements of speculative stocks. Speculation became the dominant factor in investors' entry into the market. During this period, stocks broke away from their basic book values and commanded higher and higher prices in relation to their reported earnings. We were in a market that placed premiums on exciting stocks as people combed the lists for stocks that could double or even triple in relatively short spaces of time. The quest for capital gains became a way of life for middle America; the public came back into the market.

The whole ascent (stage three) had its most powerful upthrust within sixteen years between 1950 and 1966. This period witnessed the Dow climb from the 200 level as we entered the 1950s to the 1000 mark in February of 1966. What began as an investment move in the early fifties grew into a wild speculative climax in 1966, and played a final encore in 1968 with the new-issue speculative boom. This is a progression characteristic of all grand-scale bull markets.

Stage four of this supercycle never became a full depression but came in the form of three recessions: 1966, 1970, and 1974. Altogether these recessions eliminated most of the excesses of the post–World War II boom as in succession the Dow Jones defined a major bear market in 1966, a major bear market in 1970, and a major bear market in 1974.

What is interesting about these erosive downturns is that they were followed by animate realities on the upside. We are, in fact, still in this Yo-yo trading range, which has worn out the patience of millions of investors in much the same way that the 1929–32 Depression exiled investors from the market. What the 1929 bear market did in price, the 1966 grand-scale bear market has done in time. It has managed to remove the speculative zing from the market; although the average stocks have not come down 80 or 90 percent all at once as they did in 1929, in broad price terms, the majority of stocks today have been in equally erosive grand-scale bear markets. This has been due not only to speculative inertia in stocks, but also to high interest rates. In 1978–79, "prime" bonds yielding 8 to 10 percent replaced stocks in many portfolios.

Stage Three Once Again?

The Viet Nam war became stage one of another economic supercycle. The war in Viet Nam cost trillions of dollars. This cost was predictably inflationary and motivated stage two during the early and mid-seventies, an important inflation again arriving approximately three to five years after the war reached its peak, during the Tet Offensive in 1968. During this stage two, gold soared on the world markets as the dollar sank to new lows. This is the stage from which we emerged in the late 1970s. Now, in the 1980s, we have already entered the explosive stage-three phase.

Stage three is the most powerful, profitable, and dynamic phase of the cycle. Many of the problems caused by stage two—depression, the low valuation of the dollar, inflation, the energy crisis, very low levels of credibility and confidence —have evaporated. What we will witness once the grand bull market gets under way is a return to confidence in stocks, bonds, and our economic system in massive proportions. What we predict is that the Dow Jones Averages during this period will soar.

During this phase three, we will find an important change in the character of the news background through the media. Right now the public understanding of inflation is based on extrapolation of the diminished purchasing power of the dollar. The major fallacy in this understanding is based upon the national debt. Since 1949 the national debt has soared to all-time-high levels. This debt keeps growing year after year, as the government pursues a plan of deficit spending. This deficit spending (aggravated by Viet Nam) is the cause of the present inflation, and it will continue to be a definite ingredient in future inflation. This debt, however, has bought much of the industrial strength that this country has today.

In 1949, during the post–World War II period, we found that the national debt made some very important and substantial moves to the upside. It is now at all-time highs, and each year that we pursue a course of deficit spending this debt increases. What many of those concerned about the fall of the dollar today fail to realize is that the gross national product has far outpaced the movement of the national debt to the upside. This demonstrates that our national debt has paid for a good portion of today's economic growth. In coming years we will find that most of the investments made and financed by this debt will begin to show more and more productivity, as foreign countries purchase American goods and services. It is time to realize that the economic pendulum is now about to swing dramatically to the other end of the spectrum. Capitalism will flourish.

Inflation is giving way, as it has in other periods, to a new grand-scale economic boom, and has put our economic system on the springboard to new all-time highs in productivity, growth, and profitability. The result eventually will broaden our tax base and move toward a balanced national budget. This will happen as soon as the dollar falls to a low enough level on the world markets to attract the buying of our goods and services on a broad scale.

At some time during each year from 1963 to 1979, the Dow Average has been in the 800 to 900 zone. This price range establishes a new base from which the supplies of stock have been conveyed from a generation of speculators to a new market generation of more resolute investors. In taking a grand bull market investment approach, it is important to determine, as precisely as possible, when this transition from one generation to the next is at hand.

We think that now is the time, after a depression, when the U.S. economy is poised to blossom anew. History is ready to repeat. As we enter the final decades of the twentieth century, we are due for one more grand bull market. It is important to remember that the beginning of a grand bull market starts at a time when most have forgotten how swiftly and powerfully market momentum can be generated by incoming cyclical tidal waves of prosperity. The market is now positioning itself in such a way as to delude the great mass of investors; instead, far-seeing investors are accumulating the floating supplies of desirable company shares. This is exactly the position the market should be in for a massive move to the upside.

No two decades are the same. The accumulation in the seventies generated a market that caused overlooked fundamentals to be valued at much higher prices in the eighties. The present negative economic thinking gives capital-rich investors seeking dividend yield the opportunity to accumulate high-grade investment quality stocks under the cover of weakness, and to establish rewarding speculative positions at unusually low risks in the present-day market. The dividend-conscious market we are now in is also the kind that usually exists before major and substantial upmoves. The dividend market enables investors to buy stocks and hold on to them for years, while they are receiving high yields in relationship to historically low valuations of stock prices.

PART TWO
DOWBEATER
METHODS

3

How the Rich
Get Richer!

The East-West Investment Technique

The most certain way to protect your principal in the stock market is to invest only with the interest it earns. Too often investors attempt overnight riches, failing to realize that it is not the killing which makes for market success, but rather the compounding effects that a consistent investment strategy provides over a period of years. Windfall profits mean nothing unless they are maintained and maximized. Thus, applying conservative banking principles, speculating only with interest earned by one's investment program, in the long run yields an improved return on capital in a much more consistent fashion.

Many investors aim for a 50 to 100 percent return per

year on their investments. That is, for most, too high. In reality, a 10 to 20 percent return per year on capital is sufficient to compound even small amounts of money into a plump nest egg over the course of a decade as seen from the following table.

Ten years compound gain

At an annual percent gain of	$10,000 grows to ...
0%	$ 10,000
+ 10%	25,937
+ 20%	61,917
+ 30%	137,858
+ 40%	289,255
+ 50%	576,650
+ 60%	1,099,512
+ 70%	2,015,994
+ 80%	3,570,047
+ 90%	6,131,066
+100%	10,240,000

(See Lowry Fund Eclipse Method, p. 48, for utilizing East-West plan.)

In today's bond market, yields are the highest they have been for over a century. Consequently, now is almost an ideal time to start a program of investing with principal, and speculating with interest.

Building the East Pool

The formula for speculating with interest is the basic procedure on which the super fortunes amassed in this country have been built and enhanced. The simple reason the rich get richer is that they can speculate with their interest income. Here's how *you* can use the same approach.

First of all, one must build a pool of capital consisting of ultraconservative investments. This pool of capital, which we'll call the East Pool, should be invested in bonds, blue chip equities, savings accounts, and/or short-term paper. These conservative media give investors both strong basic capital and sufficient income to keep positioned to make large returns on their more aggressive investments, while keeping their principal intact. Investors can survive a wrong decision or a series of wrong decisions because they risk only the interest on their principal, not the basic fund itself. Such a strategy eliminates that large gray area of investing in which investments seem to offer both a conservative return and the possibility for dynamic growth. This paradoxical goal often proves unattainable, and may indeed lead to serious losses.

The aggregate yield from the East Pool should be between 6 and 10 percent or more, depending upon the interest-rate structure that prevails.

A penny saved is a penny earned. Therefore, the first and foremost investment every "investor" should make in structuring an East Pool should be in a regular passbook savings account. A savings account provides investors with instant availability to their money without market depreciation and a solid building block for financial success. A savings account should be the bedrock foundation of your financial pyramid. As history has proven, a solid foundation may ultimately translate into large speculative gains.

A second vehicle for capital deployment in the East Pool is the certificate of deposit, taken on an annual basis. These notes provide the investor with slightly better yield than a savings account, and they add to the diversification of the East Pool.

Further, we recommend investing in Treasury Bills and other short-term paper. It is generally wise to buy T Bills with a six-month duration or less. That way you are not subject to interest-rate changes. The best municipal bonds to buy are those that will come due in the next three to five years. These offer a high tax-free yield, plus a return of principal as they come due. This short-term approach to municipal bonds gives the investor tax-free yield, with protection against fluctuations in the money market. These holdings may be supplemented by choice common stocks such as American Brands, American Home Products, Exxon, etc. These diversified East Pool investments give the investor a solid base that can support entry into the more speculative and, hopefully, more profitable investments. In other words, this program will generate income to continually fuel a speculative and aggressive West Pool program.

Building the West Pool

The purpose of the West Pool is to use the interest earned on principal in such a way that one dollar does the work of ten to twenty. The selection of the trading vehicles to be used in the West Pool must, therefore, be made with particular discrimination. First of all, West Pool investments must be oriented toward high leverage. While the reason for investing in the East Pool was to generate and assure a conservative return, in the West Pool investments are made ultra-aggressively, in high-risk vehicles to achieve capital gains.

However, once positions in the West Pool are closed out, profits revert to and are reinvested in the East Pool. This assures that capital deployed in the West Pool is put to work in a program designed ultimately to enhance the capital in the East Pool. As long as the East Pool is fueled with the profits from the West, the capital resources invested will continue to grow and will thus continually build a broader interest base for the investor. Such a program assures that dynamic speculative gains that may occur in the market are not frittered away but rather compounded, by recycling the aggressive speculative profits back into the conservative pool.

As long as investors limit their speculative funds to interest received, they're in a strong and relatively hazard-free position. Using the East and West Pools, investors have working for them both a defensive and an offensive strategy in their money-management program. They are able to survive speculative misfires; and even more important, they are always able to keep their basic investment capital intact.

By far the best kind of investments in the West Pool are low- and ultra-low-priced stocks. These offer the investor the potential for large speculative gains in the coming years. Now, and in the past few years, low-priced stocks have been relatively dormant. There has been little public sponsorship of these stocks. In fact, many are selling substantially below their historic levels, and in many instances below book value. This could mean that many may be poised to advance significantly.

The reason we believe this will happen is that many of these low-priced companies are in a stronger position now than they have ever been before. These companies are in a powerful position to leverage their capital through the technological advances they are making. In addition, these companies are capable of increasing their sales dramatically because of their small size relative to the industries they are in. Theoretically, it is much easier for a company to double its sales from a $25 million sales base than it is for General Motors with its sales base in the billions, which already represents 60 percent of this country's automobile industry.

These lesser companies offer high leverage and visible potential for exponential gains in the coming decade. There have been low periods in the history of the stock market which offered such excellent opportunities, at such attractive prices. Some of these shares may gain between 200 and 500 percent in market value, once the speculative fever returns to Wall Street. This fertile sector is indeed likely to spawn the companies that will be the new IBM, the new Xerox, or the new Polaroid.

Right now, most investors are asleep. We are emerging from a period of deep gloom in the stock market, a period that put maximum pressures on low-priced stocks. However, this period of gloom and lack of confidence is an ideal opportunity to build a diversified West Pool of low-priced stocks. The West Pool ought to consist of between seven and ten issues selling between $2 and $10 a share. It's from these price levels that exponential gains are most likely.

When the Dow Jones Averages climb to new all-time highs toward the 2000 level, the public will race to get back into the market. The result will be an overnight musical chairs scramble among investors seeking to buy shares of low-priced stocks. Once this speculative fever begins, it will run rampant and persist for many years. Right now, while these stocks are at such low valuations, is the ideal time to purchase them—using, of course, the dividends and interest earned in the East Pool. If you are still relatively young, supplementary income from your career can be used as a catalyst to kick off the West Pool.

There are many possible variations of the basic East and West Pool Investment Plan. The plan is obviously flexible. Make certain to keep the East Pool ultra-conservative and the West Pool ultra-aggressive. In this way you'll be protected against the inevitable shifts that occur in the market. Many will prefer to retain 50 percent of the profits in the West Pool to maximize speculative gains.

The West Pool Options Strategy

The advent of the options market has created a new investment wave. If this wave repeats the pattern of all other investment waves, most investors will not prosper but will, in the long run, lose money. This is because the options market creates the most dynamic leverage that the stock market has ever offered. Unfortunately, investors will find that leverage is a double-edged sword—the profits earned are as easily lost again, and as quickly. Today, investors can achieve leverage power of 1 to 10 through the purchase of options, and the purchasers of options have a limited downside risk, as they can only lose their initial nominal investment. This makes the option market a dynamic, potentially profitable money-management tool. With the leverage that is available in the options market, investors can make one dollar do the work of twenty. This means that investors with a one-thousand-dollar investment can control twenty thousand dollars worth of stocks for short periods of time, usually six to nine months.

An important guideline to remember is that options above $3 should usually not be purchased. There is no reason to lose more than 3 to 5 points in any speculation, and much of the leverage on an option investment is lost when an option is above $3. Profits realized in the options market should be converted to cash on a quarterly basis and reinvested in the East Pool. There are often cases in which options explode overnight.

The options market is not for beginners. The great volatility that exists within the options market exists only for the benefit—that is, the profit—of a few. Careful study and a great amount of time must be devoted before any option position is taken.

Dowbeater Option Stocks
Suggested Profit Action Possibilities
(Stock owned outright in East Pool, or stock option speculation in West Pool.)

The following is a list of diversified Dowbeater selections, recommended by the authors for long term gains. The stocks are identified in the table below by Company Name, Ticker Symbol—which identifies the stock for trading on the stock exchanges or in the Over-the-Counter market, and Price (as of 3/23/84)—which indicates the price per share of each stock.

Company Name	Ticker Symbol	Price (As of 3/23/84)
Baxter Travenol Labs	BAX	17⅛

Medical equipment and supplies.

This billion-dollar company is an ideal option stock candidate for speculators with the fortitude to buy cyclone, rollercoaster dips in BAX's price structure.

Bristol-Myers	BMY	45¼

Proprietary and ethical drug manufacturing.

This billion-dollar growth company has exceptional relative strength and has potential for both the option trader and the long-term investor.

Coca Cola   KO   54⅜
Beverages.

KO benefits from the charisma of its Coca-Cola product and the punch of a product research and marketing team that's never satisfied with just being excellent. An ideal speculation for option wildcatters (West Pool).

Community Psychiatric Centers   CMY   29
Acute psychiatric hospitals.

This exponential growth company is an excellent stock for options traders to take delivery on or for investors to just purchase at the market.

Donaldson, Lufkin & Jenrette   DLJ   15⅞
Securities, investment management, and financial services.

A takeover bride candidate for any major financial services corporation groom seeking to expand into the blossoming stock brokerage boom. A good stock for options trading or long-term investment, especially during volumes lulls and price dips on the NYSE.

Loral Corp   LOR   19⅝
Military electronics.

LOR has benefited from the new development of high-tech military electronics. LOR should provide investors long-term gain and option traders plenty of action.

Marriott Corp.   MHS   64¾
Hotels and food.

MHS and its world-renowned hotel chain can provide investors a good long-term rest for their blue-chip capital or short-term overnight accommodations for call options traders.

McDonalds   MCD   66⅝
Fast-food restaurants.

Nothing stops Ronald McDonald from being America's leading Pied Piper of the fast-food industry for young

and old and for long-term investors and option speculators who are trying to leverage their capital with Big
Mac calls.

Northern Telecom   NT   34¼
Telecommunications equipment.
NT has exceptional possibilities as a result of the blossoming telecommunications industry, with options that
could benefit from short squeezes that are bound to materialize in this high flyer of the '80s.

Toys R Us   TOY   37⅝
Toy retailer.
Toy is poised for extraordinary gains as their formula
for success of bringing children great toys at low prices
wins the hearts of millions of America's toddlers. An
ideal long-term investment or a good options trade for
those who realize that options are not toys.

The West Pool New-Issue Strategy

We are now entering a phase in American economic history,
which will require a huge influx of speculative capital. As
the market explodes on the upside, there will again (as in
the 1950s and 1960s) be hundreds of small, innovative
companies offering their shares to the public for the first
time. These companies may hold promise of new breakthroughs in technology, and some may become notably
profitable. Although investing in these companies requires
a carefully acquired and thorough understanding of the
background of each company and the industry it is a part of
before one invests, the gains from this early-entry speculation in winners can be dramatic.

So, also, can the pitfalls. One need only examine the

1962 or the 1968 new-issue boom. Ultimately both produced far more losers than gainers. On the other hand, there
is no company on the exchanges today that was not at one
time either a new issue or a spinoff of a company that was
once a new issue. Thus, the third trading vehicle recommended to complete the West Pool Investment Program is
carefully selected new issues. Chart 2, below, summarizes
the complete East-West Investment Technique.

INTEREST

WEST Pool
Fast Speculative Gain

- LOW PRICE STOCKS
  1-5 Years
- NEW ISSUES
- OPTIONS
- AGGRESSIVE STOCKS

EAST Pool
Long Term Investment Security

- SAVINGS ACCOUNTS
- TREASURY BILLS
- CERTIFICATES OF DEPOSIT
- MUNICIPAL BONDS
- MUTUAL FUNDS (Insured)
- LONG TERM INVESTMENT
  STOCK POSITIONS

PROFITS

The East-West Investment Technique

Chart 2   The East-West Investment Technique: The ultra-
conservative East Pool investment interest fuels the ultra-
aggressive West Pool; profits from the West Pool then recycle
back to the East Pool. This creates a greater base of principal,
which then returns even larger amounts of interest to the
West Pool. Even in years when West Pool speculations are
unsuccessful, the East Pool principal remains intact.

Keep in mind the fact that the technological growth of the American economy has come largely from those who are willing to speculate. Every idea, every production, every invention was someone's speculation at one point. Successful speculation requires both a vision of the future and the courage and funds to take action before an opportunity is lost. With any speculation there is, of course, no guarantee that profits will be made. The goal of any speculation is to find probably one situation out of three that will result in phenomenal rewards. There are no guarantees in any speculation except the guarantee that you can give yourself: Speculate only with interest from a fund composed of conservative assured-income securities, diversified both as to type and maturity.

Suggested Profit Action
Possibilities for the West Pool

Genetic Systems   GENS   6¼
An excellent long-term speculation on genetic engineering.

Orbit Instrument   ORBT   6¼
Electronic equipment for defense.
Don't strain your eyes trying to find a quote on the NYSE or AMEX; ORBT is hidden in the OTC section and hides the potential for ORBT to possibly soar into a new orbit with more than $3 per share in cash.

Puerto Rican Cement   PRN   8⅜
Cement manufacturing.
PRN stands to benefit from a blossoming building boom in Puerto Rico and will benefit as the largest manufacturer of cement in that region. Selling below book value of $13.75, PRN is an intriguing speculation.

4

The Two Main Methods of
Security Analysis

How to Discover Which Stocks to Buy

Over the years the procedures for security evaluation have become divided into two major categories: fundamental and technical analysis. The fundamental method is based on the theory that, over a period of time, stock prices are the slaves of earning power. Market fundamentalists gather basic statistical data about an industry and the companies within it, and from these data they rate the relative attractiveness of particular issues at their current prices. They attempt to determine whether a stock is a sound issue and if it will go higher or lower, by virtue of available statistical information.

The material (which must be constantly reviewed and updated) considered by fundamental analysts includes a company's past and current earnings; profit margins; price/

earnings multiples; earnings rates on invested capital; stockholders' equity (book value); capitalization ratio of debt to equity; current asset/liability ratios; rates of growth; taxation; cash flow; dividend policy; labor relations; expenditures for research; international business, merger, or acquisition prospects; new products, goods, or services. Market acceptance of products and reputation for quality are also important factors.

Overall fundamental factors would include the trends in a particular industry, interest and inflation rates, monetary stability, government regulation, environmental problems, and the indicated state and direction of the entire economy —recession, boom, or stagnation. Of these, interest rates are among the most important determinants because when interest rates are low, corporations can borrow economically, and individuals can borrow to buy stock. Any steep increase in interest rates has almost always depressed stock prices.

Finally, the fundamentalist will make value determinations on the quality and effectiveness of corporate managements. Are they stodgy, progressive, cost-conscious, imaginative, innovative, young, promotion-minded, or ingrown? Above all, do they own a lot of stock in the company themselves?

An ongoing coverage of the above items, developed by a constant flow of information contained in corporation interim and annual reports, provides fundamentalists with what they need to determine the desirability of a particular security. The conclusions are based on the knowledge, the experience, and the judgment of each analyst. Even with identical data, however, opposite opinions may develop; unanimous approval as to the desirability of a stock is not a frequent phenomenon among fundamentalists.

By far the greatest numbers of security analysts use the fundamental method. They are less concerned with price swings and the level and direction of the market than in significant potentials for the rise or fall in corporate earnings or dividends. Indeed, many fundamentalists believe that there is no reliable method for predicting market directions in advance. Since their research can dig up such exciting winners as Xerox, IBM, Diagnostic Data, American Brands, Limited, Inc., Metromedia, Twentieth Century Fox, 3M, and Houston Natural Gas, they also believe that outstanding earning power can and will be generously rewarded even in dull markets.

Many other market professionals, however, contend that appraisal of stocks strictly on a fundamental basis is incomplete. They insist that the market is a dual phenomenon—psychological as well as logical—and that a changing psychological climate in Wall Street can affect the prices of securities quite as powerfully as changes in earnings or dividends. Some have suggested that under "average" economic conditions the controlling factors are 60 percent fundamental or logical and 40 percent cyclical or psychological, but in the extremes of a boom or recession the ratios change drastically; the cyclical market action or response of individuals then becomes the controlling factor in influencing decisions to buy or sell to the extent of 60 percent or more.

Technical Analysis

The second major procedure in security appraisal, and more specifically directed toward market timing, is technical analysis. This system arrives at stock valuations by studying the day-by-day performance of individual stocks and the market as a whole; by carefully recording and charting the daily volumes of trading and price movements in issues. Technical analysis attempts to discern future price trends from past performance of active stocks, or from barometers such as the DJIA. The technician insists that in making determinations about a stock, a perception or reading of the prevailing trend in the market as a whole and in the particular issue is a more reliable instant guide than reported or estimated earnings or dividends.

Often markets go up or down quite dramatically, without any significant change in fundamental values. Prices are arrived at by a sort of mass movement, psychologically induced, of public money into or out of the market. The success of landings on the moon could not be evaluated by statistics or on profit-and-loss statements, but it did give great market stimulus to scientific equities. When President Kennedy died, the market sank; but it bounded back up a few weeks later when the grief of an emotion-struck nation had subsided. These sudden floods of investment capital into, and out of, the market become evident when: (1) the daily trading volume on major exchanges increases noticeably; (2) increase in volume is accompanied by new "highs" in popular issues. Conversely, when volume increases inordinately on the down side, in general, the sale of stocks is indicated and a further price decline may be expected.

To record and analyze these price and volume data, charts are essential to the technician. There are two principal kinds: *bar charts* and *point and figure charts*.

The popular bar chart may cover transactions for a day, a week, a month, a quarter, or a year. Customarily the horizontal scale on the chart, running from left to right, will represent the time scale in the period charted; the vertical scale will reflect price changes.

Plotting such a chart has become fairly standardized. One connects the day's high and the day's low by a vertical line; the closing price is indicated by a very short horizontal line crossing the vertical one. You plot in the same data for each succeeding trading day, and shortly you have a chart that reveals a trend—which is what you're looking for.

Volume is usually shown on a special scale running along the bottom of the page; and many charts also carry notes at the bottom indicating when a stock sells ex dividend or ex rights or pays an extra or stock dividend.

If you are a neat person with a mathematical turn of mind, you can plot and keep up these charts yourself. Most people, however, prefer to view such charts published along with many research studies on individual stocks in financial journals or as mailed regularly to subscribers of such services as Trendline, Mansfield, M. C. Horsey, Value Line, Standard & Poor's, etc.

These charts, properly constructed, provide valuable information. First, they reveal what people were willing to pay or accept for a given stock on any day. This price represents the ultimate value of a stock—what it will fetch in the marketplace. Emotion, caprice, or mass psychology, rather than reason, may have influenced the prices recorded; but prices do not lie. The chart reveals the "bloodless verdict of the marketplace." Never mind earnings prospects, glamour, or sponsorship—a stock is worth, on a particular day, no more and no less than what it sold for!

A succession of these weekly or monthly charts, according to technicians, should reveal a dominant directional

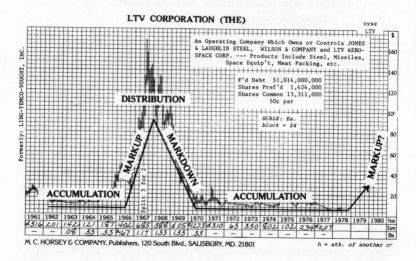

LTV CORPORATION (THE)

nyse LTV

Formerly: LING-TEMCO-VOUGHT, INC.

An Operating Company Which Owns or Controls JONES & LAUGHLIN STEEL, WILSON & COMPANY and LTV AEROSPACE CORP. --- Products Include Steel, Missiles, Space Equip't, Meat Packing, etc.

F'd Debt $1,014,000,000
Shares Pref'd 1,424,000
Shares Common 13,311,000
50c par

DISTRIBUTION

SCALE: Ea.
block = $4

MARKUP

MARKDOWN

ACCUMULATION

Split 3 for 2

ACCUMULATION

MARKUP?

	1961	1962	1963	1964	1965	1966	1967	1968	1969	1970	1971	1972	1973	1974	1975	1976	1977	1978	1979	1980	Year
Earn	d316	2.01	1.42	1.21	1.87	4.02	6.85	3.86	d.05	d.73	d3.10	.63	3.50	8.02	1.02	2.34	2.07				Earn
Div.	-	-	.08	.33	.33	h.67	1.17	1.33	1.33	.33	-	-	-	-	-	-					Div.

M. C. HORSEY & COMPANY, Publishers, 120 South Blvd., SALISBURY, MD. 21801

h = stk. of another cr

Chart 3 Bar chart of LTV: This showed the potential up-move of LTV from its years of accumulation below $20 per share. Accumulation is part of a four-stage cycle clearly identifiable on long-term monthly charts, the stages being:

1. Accumulation—(Winter) during this time, long-term investors take their positions.
2. Markup—(Spring) as a result of the sharp tightening of supplies, during accumulation prices move up. (LTV is now in this stage, identified a year ago on this chart.)
3. Distribution—(Summer) the farsightedness of the investor during the accumulation stage pays off. The news is out and the public buys and the professionals sell. (This has yet to happen.)
4. Markdown—(Fall) Distribution is now over. Price weakness sets in. The public has just bought the "good news" and the stock promptly sells off. With public now in, who is left to buy? The results: markdown in prices.

Originally recommended in the first edition of *The Dowbeaters*, and still recommended now.

trend. An upthrust may be motivated by net earnings rising significantly in each quarter, or by a general market confi-

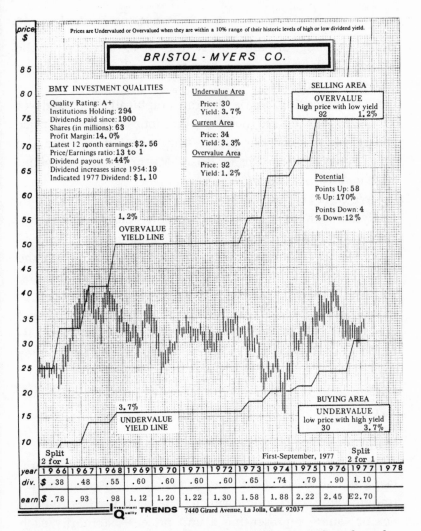

Chart 4 Bar chart of Bristol-Myers: This identifies the relationship of stock price with the fundamental parameter of dividend yield. Notice how the price finds support near its 3.7 percent historical dividend band. This very informative chart showed Bristol-Myers to be undervalued in the original edition, and has since reached the top of the band, soaring to 45 (adjusted for 2-for-1 stock split, May 1983).

dence pushing up all stocks—the weak along with the strong. A downturn may sensitively reflect a decline in investor confidence.

The preceding charts portray graphically the kinds of messages bar charts portray: the four seasons of price movement of LTV (an interesting speculation); and the price value relationships of Bristol-Myers Co. (an excellent high-quality investment).

We can't begin to cover here all the nuances of bar-chart analysis, such as reversals, breakouts, boxes, rectangles, head-and-shoulder formations, consolidations, etc. For real professional guidance in this area we urge you to get the Wycoff Course from the Stock Market Institute in Phoenix, Arizona. This can give you a basic course on the subject of charts and help you use the technical approach to detect peaks and valleys and identify patterns of supply and demand in individual stocks that may project the prices they may reach a few months hence.

● **Recommended Action:** Stock Market Institute, Phoenix, Arizona.

Point and Figure Charts

A less common, more sophisticated chart used by technicians is called the *point and figure chart,* used to reflect trading value. Here a uniform chart paper is used, with each box or square representing a unit price. Customarily each square will represent a one-point move in the price of a stock (in shares selling below 20, each box may represent only half a point). Price changes, in order to show on the chart, must cover at least three squares, up or down. If an issue continues to trade within a very narrow range, day after day, then the chart will remain unchanged. Only if the stock "breaks out" either up or down will changes actually get plotted. The letter X is customarily used to denote up moves, and O for downs. Trendlines are not drawn until a bullish or bearish formation has appeared. Then a trendline will be constructed at an angle of 45 degrees. Shares are thought to be in a buying range when transactions are above the trendline, and in a selling phase when transactions take place below.

Point and figure charts ignore the time factor, since they only reflect trading volume. Such charts may be "flat" for a week or ten days at a time, and then zig and zag like an oscilloscope within one or two active trading days. P & F charts simply record changes in price, and in this way describe those demand/supply factors affecting a particular stock that may elevate or lower its quotations. The theory is that if demand is strong (more insistent than supply) a stock will continue to go up until supply (selling pressure) emerges.

The technical theory postulates a series of market waves; and the objective is to divine by charts and their interpretation the length, height, and duration of these waves. There is evidence that institutional investors, particularly since the market debacle of 1974, have been placing increasing confidence in the prognostications of their technical analysts.

Substantial exchange firms employ technical analysts along with a battery of the fundamental variety. Among the technical virtuosi are Donald Hahn of Becker Securities Co., Chicago; Robert Farrell of Merrill Lynch; Stanley Berge of Tucker Anthony, R. L. Day; Ned Davis of J. C. Bradford, Nashville; and Gail Dudack of Pershing & Co. Many metropolitan banks have staff technicians also.

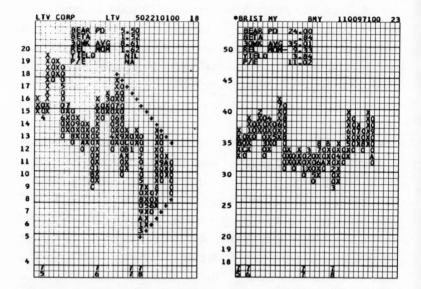

Charts 5 and 6 Point and figure charts of LTV and Bristol-Myers: These show the interacting forces of supply (Os) and demand (Xs) for these two stocks. These charts not only showed trend action, but also showed potential price objectives through a counting formula. This count shows, during areas of accumulation or distribution, the approximate potential price moves from these zones. (*Charts courtesy of Chartcraft, Inc., Larchmont, N.Y.*)

Some of these technicians have gained considerable acclaim for their accuracy in calling market turns. Aided by carefully manicured charts and precise graphs, these market "pros" have frequently accurately predicted the impact of mass psychology and its magnetic influence on security prices.

Charts identify the flow of money in and out of the market and record market volume, volatility, short sales, and the relative desirability of competing forms of investments, particularly bonds. The growth in money supply is also factored in by many technicians. They contend that the amount of money in circulation has a vital bearing on that portion that flows into securities. Declines in money supply have in recent times, quite predictably, depressed P/E multiples for stocks.

Technical analysis is a useful tool and a powerful cross-check on fundamental analysis. In the selection of Dow-beaters the fundamentals must be right—strong balance sheets, upcurves in earnings, high profit margins and high return on equity, etc., but we also like to look at a current bar chart on the issue and the Dow Averages. If these, too, are "uptick" we have welcome confirmation that the security researched is favorably positioned for current purchase. Further, we'd think twice about a recommendation if a bar or P & F chart of a stock were strongly adverse. We might still favor the stock but await a more propitious time for its purchase.

Neither basic method of stock analysis is an answer in itself. By combining the strengths of both methods new dimensions of portfolio strategy unfold. The following Dow-beater methods show how.

- **Recommended Action:** Three point reversal method of point and figure charting; A. W. Cohen, author; available at Chartcraft—Larchmont, New York

5

Lowry's Eclipse Method
of Investing

A Deductive Dowbeater-Market Timing Approach

The essential problem for any investor is identifying the times opportune for entering the bull markets while still retaining the flexibility to adjust investments during those negative periods of blind spots in the market, when stock prices erode due to bear markets or sharp panic breaks. The *eclipse method* of investing presents one way of solving this problem. The eclipse method of investing buys in the market's dark periods and sells when the crowd regains confidence, and especially overconfidence, in the market. These dark periods occur during stock-market declines, when the light of reason is blocked from the shortsighted mass-investing public.

Lowry's Reports, Inc. is probably the best guide to eclipse investing. For the past forty-six years, Lowry's Reports have been giving specific buy-and-sell advice, based on the supply-demand relationship of the entire market.

The Lowry method is based on the theory that stock prices are governed by the law of supply and demand. In other words, when there are more buyers than sellers, stocks go up. When there are more sellers than buyers, stocks go down. In order to detect the extent of buying or selling pressure, Lowry's measures both the volume (number of shares) of stocks traded daily and the total amount of gains and losses of those traded. These measurements are then plugged into a formula that, when computed, gives a buy or sell signal (Leisner, p. 67).

According to the Lowry theory,

Stocks only do two things: Their prices fluctuate Up and Down; their Trading volume increases and decreases. That is all they ever do! Thus, the action of the entire market, which includes the combined actions of insiders, professionals, specialists, mutual funds, tape readers, short sellers, fundamentalists, chartists, bulls and bears, as well as the "public" and odd-lotters, can be reduced to simply 4 basic totals:

1. Total GAINS for all round-lot (100 shares) stocks closing higher than the previous day's close.
2. The total VOLUME of transactions for stocks registering gains.
3. Total LOSSES for stocks closing lower than the previous day's close, and—
4. The total VOLUME for declining stocks (Lowry's Reports, Inc., Palm Beach, Florida, p. 3).

An examination of the results achieved with the Lowry method reveals impressive performance. A study at the Finance Department of the Wharton School of Finance and Commerce indicates:

The Lowry method of technical analysis, which utilizes only past price and volume data, led to returns of more than double those achieved by naive buy-and-hold investment programs. In addition, this performance was achieved in the face of very stringent operational limitations over a number of different time periods extending as far back as 25 years. This, of course, is an apparent contradiction of both the Efficient Markets and Random Walk theories (Roebuck and Roebuck, p. 24).

According to Paul Desmond, president of Lowry's Reports, the analysis identifies market moves in much the same way as a barometer predicts storms—a storm does not occur each time the barometer forecasts one, but there has never been a time when a storm occurred that the barometer did not indicate a storm was coming. In other words, Lowry's analysis has called many market moves that did not materialize, but there has never been a market move of major importance that was not identified in its early stages by the Lowry service. Obviously, such an indicator has great profit potential for the investor. It is no wonder that some 90 percent of Lowry's followers are professionals, and that Lowry's is one of the most respected market services available today.

Lowry's method is particularly effective when coupled with the trading of mutual funds. When mutual funds are the trading vehicle and one is using Lowry's buy and sell signals, the door is opened to exponential possibilities of compounding. The performance of mutual funds is generally good to excellent during grand-scale bull markets. During sideways or eroding markets, mutual funds' performance is generally mediocre to poor. This is because mutual funds are structured to analyzing companies and industries but not the important and broad movements in the stock market. This is where Lowry's comes in: using Lowry's for the market timing, and mutual funds for the selection of individual industries and stocks, investors have a complete investment program working for their advantage. In addition, the costs of trading no-load mutual funds is minimal. Usually these funds charge management fees of less than 1 percent per year. Shown in the table on page 52 is a hypothetical performance summary of the Lowry conversion program applied to twenty-one large mutual funds. In every case the Lowry conversion approach outperformed each fund and outperformed the Dow over the sixteen-year period.

As Paul Desmond explains it:

> Mutual funds are a $278 billion industry, and with the liquidity requirements that go along with that industry, we could see where we could be fully invested in growth securities during periods of advance. Then, when we perceived the market decline, we could immediately liquidate within a matter of hours, go into a money market fund, a totally defensive vehicle, and wait for a new buy signal . . . and for almost no cost at all. Even with a load fund, once you pay your initial entrance fee, then you can stay within that family of funds and rotate back and forth indefinitely, permanently, as long as that option is available. It might be open for the next 25 or 50 years for a $5 fee for each transaction.
>
> Now, to be able to roll a million or two or ten million dollars back and forth for $5 is no load. [No-load funds have no sales or commission charges.] IT IS NO LOAD. And in addition to the speed that you have, you have consistency. The mutual funds have a tremendous advantage over common stocks in that you can actually know with a very, very high degree of certainty before a market bottom occurs what you're going to want to be invested in. With common stocks, you just can't do that (Desmond, p. 13).

Using the Lowry buy and sell advice, the eclipse method of investing works as follows: Buy growth or aggressive growth mutual funds when Lowry's gives a buy signal; buy money market mutual funds when Lowry's gives a sell sig-

Fifteen-Year Performance Summary

January 1, 1968, DJIA at 906.84 Through February 29, 1984,
DJIA at 1154.63. Assumed investment: $1,000,000 on 1/1/68

Fund	Buy/Hold	Annualized % Return Compounded	Lowry Conversion Program	Annualized % Return Compounded
Amer Capital Comstock	4,606,379	9.9	8,492,924	14.1
Amer Capital Enterprise[3]	2,672,576	6.3	8,730,816	14.3
Chemical Fund	2,602,701	6.1	7,068,637	12.9
Colonial Growth	1,707,819	3.4	7,193,308	13.0
Dreyfus Fund	3,148,421	7.4	6,399,916	12.2
Fin Indust Income	5,663,159	11.3	7,635,370	13.4
Fin Indust Fund	3,416,534	7.9	6,215,563	12.0
Invest Co of Amer	3,836,484	8.7	7,877,879	13.6
Keystone S-3	2,733,319	6.4	8,108,750	13.8
Keystone S-4	1,824,458	3.8	12,315,439	16.8
Mass Invest Trust	2,351,257	5.4	5,168,894	10.7
National Stock	3,297,789	7.7	7,889,674	13.6
Oppenheimer A.I.M.	4,246,399	10.7	8,799,517	16.6
Oppenheimer Fund	2,006,365	4.4	8,369,224	14.0
Oppenheimer Time	2,897,465	9.1	7,686,736	18.2
Pennsylvania Mutual	2,072,699	4.6	28,019,032	22.9
Putnam Growth Fund	3,328,528	7.7	6,384,485	12.2
Putnam Investors	3,664,498	8.4	6,951,632	12.7
Seligman Common Stock[1]	4,022,071	9.0	10,975,957	16.0
Seligman Growth[2]	2,507,599	5.9	10,309,394	15.5
Windsor Fund	6,418,263	12.2	7,965,915	13.7
Average	3,286,894	7.6	8,979,003	14.5
Avg. (S & P)		6.9		

[1] Was Broadstreet Fund

[2] Was National Investors

[3] American General Capital Growth Fund, which was included in the original study, was merged into American Capital Enterprise Fund

nal. Using this approach, an investor can participate profitably in the market's major advances and remain fully protected in a cash position during stock-market setbacks.

Today, most of the major mutual funds, such as Kemper, Criterion, Oppenheimer, and Putnam, offer programs under which an investor can switch from money market funds into growth funds and back for a $5 fee. Thus, investors can take maximum advantage of different management strategies to suit their particular needs of the moment. This allows investors to switch within the same family of funds into the fund that gives them the best positions suited for the type of market environment at the specific time.

One of the foremost aspects of any successful market plan is a method of systematically cutting losses. The eclipse method of investing, using the Lowry buy signal, has preset criteria for identifying when supply is greater than demand and, consequently, when the position should be liquidated. This keeps investors from the kind of losses that cripple their portfolios to the point of inaction. The concept of buying and selling mutual funds in accordance with the Lowry's buy and sell signals has evolved over many years. The idea of switching from one fund to the next according to a preset plan eliminates a great deal of the anxiety that accompanies investing.

Another problem most investors face is finding a broadly diversified group of stocks that outperforms the general market, as measured by the Dow Jones Industrial Averages. The eclipse investment method using Lowry's approach to buying and selling mutual funds builds capital appreciation through the power of compounding. For example, using Lowry's approach from 1950 to 1983 with the Keystone S-4 fund as the investment vehicle, the investor would have realized 23.5 percent per year compounded. These hypothetical results are far superior to the results achieved if an investor bought IBM stock in 1950 and held it until 1983, reinvesting all dividends and keeping all shares after stock splits. IBM, one of the greatest growth stocks of the post–World War II period, grew at a mere 13 percent per year compounded.

Many investors find that they have neither the inclination nor the ability to follow the market on a regular basis, or to effectively employ a market timing strategy with their own investment program. Much discipline is required to stay with a structured approach to investing, such as the eclipse method.

For those investors who want to be relieved of the problems and concerns inherent in a market timing program, the Lowry Management Corporation offers its own unique open-end mutual fund and specialized managed account program. The Lowry Market Timing Fund is a professionally managed mutual fund that employs exclusively the distinctive market timing techniques developed by Lowry's Reports, Inc. Shareholders participate in the market without concern for the administrative complexities and the other problems involved with shifting investments in and out of the market to take advantage of market trends in the making.

The Lowry Market Timing Fund makes use of market analysis specifically and continually provided by Lowry to this unique mutual fund. It relieves the shareholder of the costs, work, and concerns that can typify successful market timing programs. The primary purpose of the Fund is to capitalize on major advances in the stock market and to remain liquid during major declines. The Fund endeavors to invest substantially in common stocks during periods when securities markets are deemed to be in an upward trend, and substantially in short-term money-market instruments when the stock market is believed to be in a declining phase.

According to Paul Desmond and John Smith, officers of the Lowry Management Corporation, when the Fund invests primarily in common stocks, Fund portfolio managers place emphasis on buying stocks possessing high liquidity and sound investment characteristics, in combination with a higher potential for performance than common stocks generally. Thus, the Fund is able to move in and out of the stocks in its portfolio with relative ease, without disrupting stock prices to a great degree.

When the Fund invests in money market instruments, its managers concentrate on high-quality securities with maturities of one year or less. Their strategic emphasis is on minimizing risk and maintaining a high degree of liquidity.

Another approach is for investors to place their money into an individually managed portfolio supervised by the Lowry Management Corporation. Under this program, the investor's assets are placed in a mutual fund family under a "switching" program. This way, an investor is able to participate in market advances, and then be shifted to cash when lower stock prices are anticipated. The primary objective of this approach is to avoid large losses that are produced from the devastating market declines that occur from time to time. The results are dramatic, considering that this is a conservatively based strategy. Hypothetically, an investor could have turned a $100,000 initial investment into $8,730,816 between January 1, 1968, and February 29, 1984, using such an approach—in this case, buying American Capital Enterprise at each Lowry buy signal, and switching to the money market fund at each Lowry sell signal.

● **Recommended Action:** Lowry's Reports; The Lowry Fund

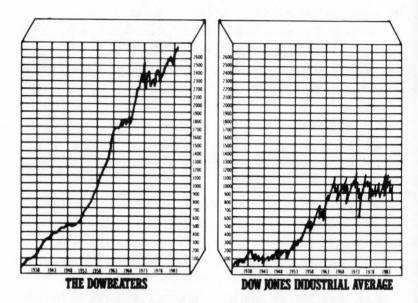

THE DOWBEATERS **DOW JONES INDUSTRIAL AVERAGE**

Chart 7 Dowbeater performance as shown on the jacket—the performance of Lowry's Reports, Palm Beach, Florida. This is a remarkable Dowbeater forecasting record that has existed throughout war, inflation, boom, depression, bear markets, bull markets, and sideways markets.

References

BISHOP, E. L. III, and J. R. ROLLINS. "Lowry's Reports: A Denial of Market Efficiency?" *The Journal of Portfolio Management* (Fall 1977), 21–27.

DESMOND, PAUL. Interview in *The Financial Planner* (October 1977), 12–15.

LEISNER, SUSAN WAGNER. "The Lowry Fund: Florida's Unique Entry in the Mutual Fund Contest," *Florida Trend* (October 1977), 67–69.

LOWRY'S REPORTS, INC. Lowry Financial Services Corp., 350 Royal Palm Way, Palm Beach, Fla. 33480. 1970.

PETERS, JOHN. "The Lowry Legacy: What He's Left May Lead to Astonishing Stock Profits for Some," *The Florida Times-Union Jacksonville Journal* (July 24, 1977), Section H. p. 1.

6

The Herzfeld Hedge:
Recovering a Billion Dollars
in Asset Value

An Inductive Dowbeater-Market Timing Approach

A major phenomenon of the market that many investors overlook is the tendency of the Dow Jones Averages to mirror the performance of the Standard & Poor's 500 Index. So closely do they correspond that it is difficult to tell which is which, when comparing them. This indicates that the performance of a portfolio of thirty stocks is almost identical over a period of time to a portfolio of five hundred stocks. In fact, once most portfolios reach a variety of more than about a dozen stocks overall, performance seems to be virtually locked into the performance of the Averages.

With this in mind, it is easy to see why it is probably better for an investor to shop for a portfolio rather than build one. Closed-end funds are ideal for this purpose because they consist of portfolios of high-quality investment grade stocks that often can be purchased at discounts from asset values. To elaborate:

Unlike regular open-end mutual funds, closed-end funds issue fixed numbers of shares and do not continuously redeem their shares. Instead of buying and selling shares directly from mutual fund companies, investors in closed-end funds must buy and sell their shares through the exchanges. The only way to buy a closed-end fund is from a selling stockholder, not directly from the fund, as in open-end funds. The only way to sell a closed-end fund is to someone interested in buying the shares in the open market; they are not redeemed at their net asset value as in open-ends. In addition, since most closed-end funds are listed on an exchange, they can be traded on margin; open-end funds cannot be traded on margin.

Prices for closed-end funds are determined by the balance of supply and demand, not their net asset value. The result is that there are often times when a portfolio of blue-chip stocks that is of equal quality to the portfolio of an open-end fund can be purchased at bargain prices. These opportunities are due to short-term market factors. When these funds are being sold at steep discounts from their net asset value, they are an ideal way by which to beat the market averages.

The discount is the difference between the market price of the investment company's stock and the asset value of its underlying portfolio. Several funds are now selling at a discount from net asset value. According to Thomas J. Herzfeld, the leading authority on closed-end funds,*

There are some objective reasons why a fund should sell at a discount. For instance, a few of the funds have unrealized capital gains which, when realized and distributed, would result in a tax liability for the stockholders. It is interesting, however, that some of those funds are selling at a smaller discount than are funds with relatively small or no unrealized capital gains. Other reasons for discounts include: disappointment with performance, lack of sponsorship (most brokers recommend funds where there is higher compensation), and tax selling.

Closed-end funds do not always sell at discounts. During periods of market speculation, such as that which occurred in 1968, many were sold at net asset value and some at a small premium. Some funds are currently selling at premiums. Examples are ASA and sometimes Petroleum Corp.

Two additional factors must be considered regarding the performance of closed-end funds: first, the commission, which for a $10 stock would be about one-half point for a round trip. Second and more important is the movement of the discount. As Herzfeld points out, "Each funds tends to have its own normal discount.

"The basis for the determination of the discount is essentially to construct a moving average of the fund's discount

---

*Thomas J. Herzfeld is president of the Miami-based firm of Thomas J. Herzfeld & Co., Inc., the only securities firm specializing in the field of closed-end funds. Mr. Herzfeld is considered to be the leading authority on the subject of closed-end funds. He is the author of *The Investor's Guide to Closed-End Funds* (McGraw-Hill, 1980), coauthor of *High-Return, Low-Risk Investment* (G. P. Putnam's Sons, 1981, Mentor Paperback, 1983), and contributing author to *The Encyclopedia of Investments* (Warren Gorham & Lamont, 1982).

and then adjust the figure based on eighteen variables. Some of the variables, of course, are given more weight than others.

"The key factor is to buy only when the discount is excessively large. Although 'excessively large' varies from fund to fund, for aggressive accounts, 'excessively large' would usually be a 5 percent deviation beyond its normal discount; for conservative accounts, this would usually mean a 10 percent deviation beyond normal.

"With the net asset value (NAV) at $10 and the discount at 30 percent (10 percent deviation), after commission of one-quarter point, the purchase price would be $7.25 ($10 minus 30 percent discount, plus one-quarter point commission). If the Dow then moved to 1100, the NAV would probably move to approximately $11. During this rise, the discount would tend to 'normalize' to 20 percent, or perhaps swing to the narrow side, to 10 percent. Discounts of closed-end funds often narrow, beyond 'normal,' in rising markets because of investor confidence and/or enthusiasm. When the fund is sold, with the Dow then being at 1100, the net price may be 9⅝. Computed as follows: NAV $11, minus discount of 10 percent, equals $9.90, less one-quarter point commission, would be 9⅝. The profit would have been 2⅜ points or 32.8 percent during a 10 percent rise in the market.

"If the market had declined 10 percent from 1000 to 900, the following may have occurred: With the Dow at 1000 we would have paid $7.25, as in our previous example. After the Dow declines to 900, the NAV would be approximately $8. The discount may have normalized to 20 percent. At a 20 percent discount, the price would be $7.20, minus a one-quarter point commission, netting $6.95—a net loss of $.30, or about 4 percent.

"*Caution:* what I have described in this example is what could happen, not what always *does* happen. However, a 20 to 30 percent profit objective, given a 10 percent rise in the Dow, would not be an unreasonable objective.

"For an actual example of what was just described, the reader can examine the movement of Madison Fund (MAD).

"In December of 1975, MAD was selling at 8⅝ and its NAV was $12.67. It was selling at the necessary deviation from its 'normal discount,' the discount then being 31.9 percent, to be bought for aggressive accounts. The Dow then

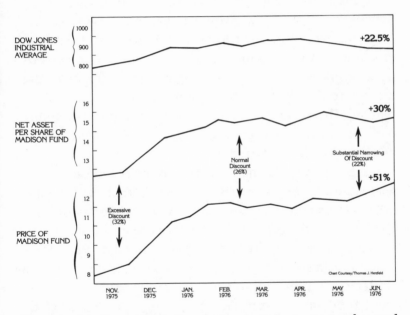

Chart 8 Madison Fund: In relation to its net asset value and the Dow Averages, this shows the performance possible during market upmoves. Conversely, during market declines, buying at substantial discounts below net asset value provides an important cushion from market setbacks.

stood at 818. During the next five months, the Dow rose 22.5 percent to 1002. The NAV of MAD rose to $16.52, or a 30 percent increase. As the market climbed, the discount narrowed to about 20 percent and the price of MAD went to $13, a gain of 51 percent, while the Dow gained 22.5 percent. The above 51 percent gain does not include the $.30 in dividends paid during the period, nor does it assume any leverage (margin) which would have brought the profit to over 100 percent.

"In summary, closed-end funds offer very superior capital gains potential in the rising markets, combined with a possible cushion if the investor misjudges the market and buys into what turns out to be a declining market. A word of caution: if the "normal" discount is not judged correctly, it can work as much against the investor as for him. Also, not all funds' NAVs move exactly proportionately to the market. Therefore, it is essential for a trader to be familiar with the historical performance and current portfolios of any fund he considers trading."

A good low-risk approach for investors whose primary goal is income exists in closed-end funds that have income-oriented portfolios. These funds pay sometimes as much as 7–10 percent per year; their portfolios consist of bonds, convertible bonds, or utility stocks. Most of the time these funds also sell at discounts, just as the stock funds do. The same strategies that are outlined for stock funds also exist for income funds as a result, i.e., the savings as a result of the discounts can be used in the same way that they are used in stock funds.

The risks in this program are less than the risks for owning a portfolio of high-grade bonds because the portfolio is bought at a discount. The only time to be cautious of bond funds is naturally during periods of generally rising interest rates.

The strategy can result in profits of 20 percent per year (market profit plus dividend) instead of 8 percent. This can be done if the fund is bought and held until the discount narrows.

There is, of course, more to successful trading of closed-end funds than just being a discount follower. According to Herzfeld, the discount is the first of nearly 20 variables that must be examined. The others are:

1. Comparison of the quality and liquidity of the fund's portfolio with other closed-end funds;
2. Evaluation of the price movements of the fund in rising and declining markets;
3. Rating of the fund's performance;
4. Yield;
5. Does it have an automatic dividend reinvestment plan? Evaluation of that plan;
6. The disposition of the fund's portfolio in the current weak or strong groups;
7. Is the capital structure leveraged or not?
8. Management fee;
9. Portfolio turnover;
10. Volatility;
11. Is it a takeover candidate?
12. Is it likely to open end?
13. Reputation of the management;
14. Mutual fund redemptions;
15. Herzfeld Index changes:
16. Does it trade on the NYSE, ASE, or OTC?
17. Number of funds with similar objectives;

18. Unrealized capital gains in portfolio;
19. International discount inefficiencies; and
20. Currency trends.

Herzfeld's activities are not limited to the U.S.; he trades the global closed-end fund market. The following excerpt from his recent speech to the NYSSI is very insightful:

"Why should closed-end traders look overseas and why at this time? Think back for a moment to the spring of 1983, specifically to the early morning of March 31st. Suddenly oil prices stabilized after their long decline. Great Britain set its North Sea oil price at $29.50 a barrel, 50 cents below its previous level. U.S. analysts had widely been projecting a one-dollar- to two-dollar-a-barrel cut. It was immediately evident on Wall Street that there was going to be a play in the oil stocks. I would like to share with you how, as a closed-end fund trading firm, we reacted to this development and how we took advantage of this opportunity by looking to the overseas closed-end funds.

"A check with our broker on the floor of the New York Stock Exchange, before the opening, told us there were buyers across the board in oils. Most major oils were going to open a point or two higher. Could we find a fund to buy that morning that specialized in oils? There is, indeed, a well-known, widely followed U.S.-based fund, whose net asset value is published weekly, specializing in the oil and energy sector. That fund is Petroleum and Resources (PEO). Many closed-end fund traders jumped into PEO that morning, and it was up about two points by the end of the trading session. Although we like PEO and consider it well-managed, we had immediately eliminated it from consideration that morning because it was selling at a premium above net asset value. PEO is perceived by most U.S. investors to be unique, the only fund specializing in the oils, and for that reason, it rarely trades at a wide discount. But, in fact, PEO is *not* the only closed-end fund specializing in the oils. We have identified and currently monitor seven other *U.K. funds* whose portfolios are dominated by oil issues. They are: Viking Resources, Winterbottom Energy, New Darien Oil Trust, Oil and Associated Investment Trust, City and Foreign Investment Trust, North Sea Assets, and T. R. Natural Resources. We also looked at the Canadian oil specialists that morning. Our next consideration, after isolating those funds most sensitive to oil pricing, was to analyze their respective discounts from NAV. For in addition to the 24 closed-end fund variables we track, it is *discount analysis,* both the historic and current discount from NAV, that is weighted most heavily in all of our trading decisions. Funds are purchased when we consider the discount to be 'excessive.' Under most circumstances, we are buyers of stock funds when they are trading at discounts five percentage points greater than normal. Conversely, we are sellers when discounts are five percentage points less than normal. A check with our broker on the floor of the London Stock Exchange, where 200 of the 340 closed-end funds we monitor trade, and a quick analysis of the NAVs which we track daily, focused our attention on Viking Resources that morning.

"Viking was 100 percent invested in the oil and energy sector, *with 88% of its portfolio invested in U.S. issues. And this is significant because there is no reason why a U.K.-based fund could not be totally invested in U.S. issues.* Indeed, some are. Viking was selling at a discount of four percentage points greater than 'normal,' at an unusually wide 32 percent discount from NAV. That compared to a 3 percent premium above NAV for PEO, the more widely known U.S.-based fund. It was additionally important to look to the U.K. because we further reasoned that with oil prices firming, the pound would strengthen against the dollar. Therefore, before the New York opening that morning, we were a buyer of U.S. oil issues, in pounds sterling, via Viking Resources on the London Stock Exchange at a 32 percent discount below the value of its portfolio.

"Within three months, the advantages of our decision were evident in three distinct areas: First, oil stocks rallied and consequently the NAVs of the oil specialist closed-end funds rose sharply. Second, in a typically repetitive pattern, as enthusiasm for the group gained momentum, Viking's discount from NAV narrowed from 32 percent to 24 percent, as its prise rose from 63P to 88P. Third, the oil price stability was obviously good news for the U.K., and sterling improved against the dollar from $1.48 to $1.53. Although we were a scale seller of Viking during the three months period, it is interesting to note that the percentage increase in dollar terms was 48 percent for Viking versus 24 percent for PEO, whose premium above NAV eroded."

There is a total of over $6 billion of assets existing between the present prices of all the closed-end funds and their net asset value. Obviously, then, closed-end funds have tremendous advantages both for the long-term investor and for trading purposes.

Business Week Letter, in an interview with Herzfeld, summarizes the advantages of trading closed-end funds as follows:

1. Closed-end funds also can offer more protection than an individual stock in a down market. If you buy a fund which is selling at an excessively sharp discount from

net asset value, a decline in the stock market will probably have little effect on the market price of the fund. That's because the fund is selling at a discount from the assets in its portfolio—and hence the assets have to fall dramatically to affect the market price of the fund.

2. Even more important is the leverage which closed-end stock funds give investors. Investors who buy wisely could outperform the market averages by a ratio of at least 2–3 times. As the stock market rallies, not only will the assets in the portfolio move, but the discount from net asset value will probably shrink. That's because investors tend to get more enthusiastic about funds during a rally—and hence bid up their prices.

3. Even if the assets in the fund's portfolio don't increase during the rally, investors can make a sizeable profit. Take a fund which has a net asset value of $10 a share, but is selling for $7—an excessively large 30 percent discount from net asset value. If that discount shrinks to only 10 percent (not an unreasonable expectation during a rally) the fund's shares would jump to $9, giving you a 30 percent return on investment.*

*Kiril Sokoloff. "The Open End in Closed-End Stock Funds," *The Business Week Letter* (29 November 1976).

● **Recommended action:**

ASA   NYSE-ASA   63½

ASA invests in South African gold mining companies. This stock has call and put options available, making it a popular vehicle for those interested in gold.

Canadian General Investments Ltd.   TSE-CGI   28¾ Canadian Dollars

Canadian General invests in a conservative portfolio of North American companies.

The stock trades at a 30 percent discount. The current relationship of Canadian dollars to American dollars gives U.S. investors a double discount.

Baldwin Securities ASE-BAL 8⅛

This company has a diversified portfolio of better quality stocks (IBM is the largest position) as well as a position in gold and silver bullion.

Closed-end fund followers have often considered this fund a candidate for liquidation. However, management has denied that a liquidation of the company is being considered. The current discount of 25 percent makes this stock attractive.

Bancroft Convertible Fund ASE-BCV 22⅜

Bancroft is a well-managed fund with a portfolio consisting of convertible bonds and convertible preferred stocks. The company is sitting on a large unrealized capital gain, and the discount is the widest among convertible bond funds.

John Hancock Income Securities NYSE-JHS 12⅝

JHS is one of the larger and better managed bond funds. Fifty-eight percent of the portfolio is rated A or better. In addition, their expense ratio is a favorable .7 percent of assets versus a group average of .89 percent. The current yearly dividend of $1.55 makes the yield 12.3 percent.

For further reading:

HERZFELD, THOMAS J. *The Investor's Guide to Closed-End Funds —The Herzfeld Hedge.* McGraw-Hill, 1980. Distributed by Thomas J. Herzfeld & Co., Inc., 7800 Red Road, South Miami, Florida.

HERZFELD, THOMAS J., AND DRACH, ROBERT F. *High-Return, Low-Risk Investment—Combining Market Timing, Stock Selection and Closed-End Funds.* G. P. Putnam's Sons, 1981, Mentor Paperback, 1983.

PART THREE
DOWBEATER
INVESTMENTS

7

The Specific Selection

of Dowbeater Stocks

Investment philosophy, with respect to common stocks, has changed notably in the twentieth century. In the early 1920s few utility stocks outside of AT&T and Consolidated Edison were included among the elite blue chips. The favorite shares then were U.S. Steel, Pullman Company, New York Central, Pennsylvania Railroad, Union Pacific, American Tobacco, Allied Chemical, and General Motors. The stress was on seasoned shares of great companies and dividend dependability. The expression "growth stock" was not yet in the financial vocabulary.

By the end of the 1920s, however, market preferences had changed. Not just the rich, the prudent, and the thrifty were stock buyers, but a whole new postwar generation of speculators entered "the market." They cared little about dividend income; they wanted to run a modest stake into a

71

killing by active speculation in what proved, from 1926 to 1929, to be a roaring bull market. Many lacked the resources, the knowledge, or the experience to trade or invest in stocks intelligently; but they were caught up in the market mania. And it took so little money to get started! In that era you could buy $1000 worth of stocks with only a 10 percent margin ($100).

Stocks seemed to go up every day. The active favorites on the Big Board were Radio Corp. (the technology company of the era, comparable with Zenith, TRW, or Motorola today), Montgomery Ward, Technicolor (which went over $100 in 1929 and sold at $1 in 1933); and over-the-counter bank and insurance shares. National City Bank reached $540 in 1929. The "new game in town" was in utility holding companies. Middle West Utilities, Cities Service, North American Company, Utilities Power & Light, and Associated Gas & Electric all zoomed to giddy heights on highly pyramided capitalizations.

The crazy game ended in 1932 with the DJIA at 42, down from 340 in 1929. Hundreds of thousands of individuals were wiped out when stock prices plummeted. They couldn't answer the "margin calls" for more money or collateral and were swiftly sold out, with each distressing day of liquidating sending the market lower. There was a short-lived bounce back in 1930, but then the Depression set in with a vengeance, bottoming out in 1932. It was not until twenty years later that the memory of this debacle was sufficiently erased, and conditions sufficiently improved, to once again attract middle-class America back into the stock market.

In the era after World War II, confidence and enthusiasm slowly rekindled. Major technological advances brought forth fabulous new industries: television, computers, data processing, wonder drugs, air conditioning, copying machines, jet planes, air transport companies, atomic power, etc. A whole new industrial world was born. Stock investing in the 1950s was not primarily for income, but for long-term gain via "growth stocks," which retained and plowed back earnings rather than distributing cash dividends. Investors in growth stocks were generously rewarded by frequent extra dividends in stock and split-ups; and by occasional dramatic rises in share prices. The market darlings of the 1950s included Columbia Broadcasting, Trans World Air, Xerox, IBM, Admiral, Zenith, Merck, Pfizer, Denison Mines (uranium), Boeing, Douglas Aircraft, G.D. Searle, 3M; and life insurance stocks: Franklin, National Life & Accident, Republic National, etc.

Later favorites from the 1960s to date would include convenience foods: Kentucky Fried Chicken, McDonald's, Howard Johnson; motel chains: Marriott, Ramada, Hilton, Sheraton, Holiday Inns; and zooming and plunging equities like Winnebago (motor homes), Levitz (furniture), and Hy-Gain (CB radios). Perkin-Elmer, bank holding companies: Frank B. Hall, Marsh & McLennan (insurance brokerage), and (since 1972) gold stocks were all winners.

The market panorama is ever-changing, with the favorite of one decade often the "dog" of the next. Some of these swings and preferences are capricious; others are dictated by changed economic conditions and visible declines in the profitability of particular industries. Caprice (and high gasoline prices) battered motor-home companies in the 1970s; low cost and hungry copper-producing countries—Peru, Chile, and Zaire—knocked down copper prices to the anguish of Kennecott, Asarco, Texgulf, Hecla, etc.; and overbuilding, as well as overmortgaging made real-estate investment trusts a disaster area. The fashionable stocks of bygone years may no longer prove desirable or rewarding. A new approach, consideration of newer industries, and a more incisive analysis of corporate managements may now be required.

Many corporations that earned well in the past now have "tired" managements. Further, diversification, which used to be so revered in security accounts, is less valued today. What counts is not how many issues you hold but how dynamic they are! For any portfolio up to $250,000 ten issues, if they are well screened, should prove adequate. Diversification is not a sacred ritual. It was merely designed to assure: (1) that a single unfortunate investment would not demolish one's net worth, and (2) some breadth of representation in sound companies in different economic sectors, so that if stocks in one industry were in a profit slowdown, other issues owned might offset declines in value or dividends by their superior performances.

We hold to no fixed points such as that some percentage of a portfolio should be in utilities, so much in industrials, so much in insurance or banking, so much in bonds, etc. We definitely take the view that the quality of the company and its potentials for rising profits and dividends are more important than general selection of securities by the industries they are in. Obviously, however, we would favor companies in promising rather than declining economic sectors.

With this background reference, we are now ready to set down some useful criteria for Dowbeater stocks, and to follow with a screened list of diversified securities meeting, in most particulars, these time-tested specifications.

A Dowbeater stock should be: (1) in a significant company (but not necessarily the leader in its industry) and in a visible or anticipated uptrend (this includes turnaround situations); (2) increasing its revenues at the rate of at least 15 percent annually; and its net profits at a rate of 12 percent or higher; (3) showing a return of 15 percent or more on stockholders' equity (book value); (4) capitalized no higher than 25 percent in long-term debt, with 75 percent equity; (5) established for at least five years; (6) grossing at least $5 million annually; (7) displaying energetic, innovative, and cost-conscious management; (8) substantially stock owned by officers and directors (20 percent or more) to properly motivate management and to fend off unwanted takeover bids; (9) owned by at least 1000 stockholders to assure reasonable marketability (the number of stockholders should be on the increase); (10) able to show a record or capability of rising dividend payments in cash, stock, or both; (11) known for the quality of its products or services, and absence of hazard or risk to users (product liability); (12) excellent in research and development of new or improved products or services; (13) free from foreign competition; (14) low cost in labor (low percentage labor to gross revenues and, preferably, nonunion to assure quality controls and insure against costly strikes that delay deliveries to customers); (15) market-sponsored by original underwriter, responsible broker/dealers, or effective floor broker (if issue is listed), any of whom may supply current information about the company to investors and to the financial community; and (16) in the case of natural resources companies, able to show ample proven reserves of petroleum, minerals, or timber.

Further, to be an attractive purchase, the issue under consideration should be available at or below ten times earnings, and below its book value.

Common stocks that qualify in most of these respects should prove acceptable purchases, under average market conditions.

Timing of the actual purchase should be checked by references to the altitude of the DJIA, possibly a Dow Theory chart, or a bar chart showing the current technical position of the stock, its indicated trendline, and trading volume. If an issue closes higher for several days in a row on large and rising volume, it is thought to be under accumulation. On the contrary, if it sells at lower closing prices for several days running, the issue may be under liquidation, and purchase, however fundamentally indicated, may be prudently deferred.

These criteria are by no means absolute and unwavering. The characteristics of winning stocks are market recognition and sponsorship. These elements are generated not only by traders, customers' brokers, and analysts, but from reports and write-ups by brokerage houses and investment advisory services; and from items, comment, or even feature articles in the *Wall Street Journal, Barron's, Forbes, Fortune,* the *Market Chronicle,* the *Financial World,* and the financial pages of metropolitan dailies.

Once a stock gets popular (by recognition and sponsorship) it may increase its times/earnings multiple at a notably faster rate than gains in its net profits and become a trading favorite. Over the long run, stock prices are the slaves of earning power. Don't expect a stock to move up with animation unless its earnings also are moving up. Past earnings and earlier "highs" for the stock are not necessarily reliable guides as to future performance.

There are six essential elements in any investment program that you should keep constantly in mind.

1. Safety of principal (avoidance of loss);
2. Income (rate of return and its dependability);
3. Marketability or liquidity (swift convertibility into cash);
4. Diversification (the spreading of risk);
5. Potential for gain; and
6. Tax bracket status.

Every investment you make can be related to these criteria. For example, government bonds rate high in liquidity, and mining stocks, low. The greatest safety of principal is, of course, in an insured bank account, insulated against any loss; whereas all marketable securities can vary—a little or a lot—in the prices they will fetch if sold. Bonds will go up or down based on prevailing interest rates; stocks will tend to follow earnings and dividends; and the level of the Dow Jones Average.

Decide what your dominant investment goals are and determine whether you are conservative, middle-of-the-road, or a daring risk taker. That way the securities you assemble may reflect, and be consonant with, your personality and goals.

Most people benefit from putting their securities in compartments—a group for long-term holding (IRA and Keogh accounts) and a cluster of speculative ones. You may be especially interested in our East-West formula, described in chapter 3. This is a flexible procedure whereby you put seasoned stocks, prime bonds, or short-term securities for permanent or "core" holdings into one group, and apply income from this fund to grubstake the purchase of more risky but presumably gainful securities with a greater market volatility. You decide in advance whether your dominant motive is for protection of capital and provision for assured income, or a drive for speculative gain, then adjust your percentage of East-West holdings accordingly.

Earlier in this chapter we outlined useful criteria for the selection of individual securities and the avoidance of underperforming stocks. Now we move from the specific to the general, and define a long-range program that may build your net worth by reinvesting income and profits. We divide your portfolio into two sections: long-term holdings for market stability and sustained income—"core" holdings in the East Pool Fund; and a trading fund comprised of more speculative securities—the West Pool Fund. The proportion of surplus resources devoted to each depends on your own age, family needs for housing, education, leisure, and health care; the level of your income; and your own temperament.

If you are a nervous, worrisome, or dubious soul, then concentrate on the East Pool and speculate only in securities of moderate risk, such as convertible bonds. If you are bold, daring, or sporting, then you can employ a higher percentage of assets in speculation and operate in low-priced stocks, warrants, reorganization issues, and, on rare occasions, options.

Investment policy is, very importantly, a matter of age. The older you are the more you need to assure safety of principal and reliability of income. Particularly if you are in the retirement years, you cannot afford high-risk commitments because, if you lost heavily, you would have neither the time nor the higher income (of earlier life) to make up for a costly "turkey."

In general, a percentage of at least 75 percent to 80 percent of blue-chip Dowbeaters in the East Pool (core holdings) would be suggested; and 20 percent to 25 percent in promising Dowbeater speculations (West Pool). In the first group there will be very little buying and selling. Indeed, the "core" stocks and bonds you own should be of such nature and quality as to produce dependable dividend increases or stock dividends to enhance income and build your capital.

In the business of investment selection and portfolio management there are broad differences of opinion, and your own judgment may well be equal, or superior, to the experts'. To illustrate: if you were to go to, say, six major brokerage firms with a request for a list of ten stocks for permanent holding, you would get six almost totally different lists—no two alike, and with little duplication of individual recommendations.

What we are saying is that prudent investment involves common sense. If you follow economic developments by reading such publications as *Barron's, Forbes, Business Week,* the daily financial page, or the *Wall Street Journal,* your own perceptions will guide you to good stocks. If you drive a Chevrolet or a Buick, you must recognize the stature of General Motors. If you see oil prices rising, you will avoid airline stocks and favor, among utilities, those using coal and hydroelectricity for power generation. (Montana Power, for example.)

Keeping up with current news can lead to rewarding security selection. You don't need to spend hours in a stock-broker's office watching the ticker to be a winning investor.

In addition to your segregation of marketable assets into two sections, and keeping informed by reading relevant periodicals, there are some axioms, adages, and instructions gleaned from the Wall Street milieu that may facilitate critical decisions about timing—when to buy or when to sell. Many old-timers contend that market timing is more important than security selection in successful trading.

Here are some of our favorite East Pool Dowbeater stocks, and some sample Dowbeater portfolios:

Emerson Radio   EME   7⅛
Manufacturing consumer audio equipment.
This low-priced stock is on the launching pad for a trip potentially to the teens in the years ahead.

Facet Enterprises   FCT   12⅞
Auto parts and equipment.
This exceptional growth stock has earnings that have doubled for the last three years and a stock price that is still under book value of $14.79.

First Executive   FEXC   12
Life insurance holding company.
A very special OTC growth company, FEXC is still a bargain, selling near book value and within striking distance of an all-time high.

Hunt Manufacturing   HUN   18¾
Art and office supplies.
HUN has just moved into the spotlight and is now traded on the NYSE. HUN should now explode into fresh all-time highs as Wall Street races to acquire the shares of this highly profitable, superperformance stock.

Limited Inc.   LTD   21½
Retail stores.
LTD is a spectacular, dynamic action performance stock whose rapid growth is now beginning to attract a broad following not only in shopping malls but on ticker tapes and quote machines across America.

Stride Rite   SRR   19¾

Children's shoes.

A high-quality investment company, SRR is prepared to walk higher as the new baby boom takes foot.

Beatrice Foods   BRY   31¼

Dairy and grocery products.

BRY is setting new highs in sales and earnings after a decade of reconsolidation. Its future growth will gain its strength from this extensive foundation.

Cox Communications   COX   40¼

Cable TV, broadcasting and publishing.

A blue chip that has immediate potential as a takeover candidate or an exceptional holding for the possibility of the stock visiting the more than $100 per-share level this decade.

Dun & Bradstreet   DNB   56

Business information, publishing, and TV.

DNB is an excellent blue-chip-quality growth stock selection for the years ahead. Buy and hold.

Fort Howard Paper   FHP   51

Paper products.

FHP continues to increase its sales earnings and dividend payout—pleasing shareholders with a stock price that parallels this growth, and hitting new high prices almost every year.

General Cinema   GCN   35½

Movie theater chain and beverages.

GCN is a great stock for investors who like movies, non-alcoholic beverages, and growth that seems never-ending.

Hartmarx   HMX   25½

Retail stores.

HMX selling at near book value of $21.37 is vastly under-valued and should prove rewarding when the price of the stock reflects its strong earnings gains.

Pall Corp.   PLL   29¾

Filters and fluid-control equipment.

PLL is an exceptional long-term holding that should benefit from increased industrial demand from the boom that is developing.

Pillsbury   PSY   35⅝

Food.

PSY is popping fresh into new all-time highs as a result of gains in Burger King and other divisions. Long-term investors can have it their way by buying and holding for the years ahead.

Saga Corp.   SGA   28½

Food serving.

SGA has fed its shareholders very well—rewarding their insight with its exponential growth. Ideal for investors.

Syntex   SYN   38½

Pharmaceuticals.

SYN is our foremost favorite pharmaceutical company, with a strong research and development budget, record sales, earnings, and dividends. Investors and option traders should keep tabs on this very special situation.

Texas Oil and Gas   TXO   23¾

Oil and gas.

TXO is set for new record highs as it consolidates in a stronger position than most of its other oil-and-gas company cousins. An ideal investment or options trade for speculators who like to stay on the wild side of Wall Street.

US Tobacco   **UBO**   **36**

Tobacco.

UBO has grown continually and is now smoking at all-time highs. An excellent Dowbeater selection.

WE ADVISE ALL READERS: IT SHOULD NOT BE ASSUMED THAT SPECULATIONS LISTED ABOVE WILL BE UNIFORMLY PROFITABLE!

🄱

Bank Stocks as
Dowbeaters

Curiously, most books on common stock investments pay little attention to bank shares, yet they rank among the oldest and most desirable of equities both for dividend income and dependable growth. Well-chosen bank shares, particularly those located in sections of the country displaying rapid economic growth, are gainful securities capable of outpacing the DJIA year after year.

In 1983 hundreds of banks reported record deposits and earnings. The NASDQ Bank Index showed a 30.30 percent gain in the value of bank stocks in 1983, contrasted with a rise of only 17.27 percent in the S&P 500 Index. The firm of Moseley, Hallgarten, Estabrook and Weeden, Inc. has tracked a group of sixty-seven regional bank stocks. These recorded an average gain of 41 percent for 1983. This beats our Dowbeater performance goal of 30 percent annually. Moreover, the 41 percent gain of these regionals does not include dividends received.

The momentum in banking should continue in 1984, and we have identified some issues that may become Dowbeaters. They'll be outlined later in this chapter; but first you ought to have some valid benchmarks or criteria so that you can judge for yourself whether a given bank share is worth buying.

In general (under conditions prevailing early in 1984), a bank stock to merit consideration should: (1) be selling at six times its earnings, (2) be selling near or below book value, (3) yield around 5 percent on its current dividend, (4) pay out 35 percent of net in dividends, (5) earn at least 8/10 of 1 percent on average assets, (6) earn 15 percent on its average equity, (7) have an equity equal to at least 5½ percent of average assets. Further, its deposits should be growing at an annual rate of 12 percent or better. These are not absolutes, but you will find that superior performing bank shares will meet most of these requirements. The most profitable banks are those with the best managements, and these ratios are valid criteria for both security and management appraisals.

Holding companies now enable bank affiliates to engage in factoring, mortgage banking, leasing, insurance, real estate, etc. Commercial banks are penetrating electronic banking and equity participations in real estate ventures and gaining access to general insurance business, securities business (including underwriting and discount brokerage), and interstate banking.

Some banks have already bought discount brokerage firms, and there is a wide move for holding companies to buy banks in other states where they are legally permitted to do so. In New England, a bank in Massachusetts can own a bank in Rhode Island or Maine. NCNB, perhaps the most progressive bank in North Carolina, and Northern Trust of Chicago, bought banks in Florida before a law was passed there forbidding commercial bank purchase and operation by "outsiders." The Bank of New York has filed an application to acquire Northeast Bancorp of Stamford, Connecticut (parent of Union Trust, with sixty branches) at a price equal to 1.85 percent of Northeast book value. First Interstate, a California bank, has licensed that name to twenty-one banks in other states, and made available computer and other banking facilities that may be shared by all members of the group.

There is, indeed, a strong trend toward interstate banking that should be considered by all bank stock investors. An acquiring bank may rapidly expand its services and its deposits, and penetrate market areas in the most rapidly growing states. For the smaller regional bank there may be a golden day ahead when the institution is sought by a major metropolitan bank at a premium price. You will doubtless recall, in your own community, a bank that sold out recently to a much larger one, creating either plump capital gains for selling stockholders, or the receipt of new shares worth a lot more than the original holdings. Most banks today are quoted around book value. A "takeover" offer, however, may be made as high as 1½ to 2 times book value. There are hundreds of banks that may become "merger bait" in 1984–85, so keep on the lookout for modestly priced regional banks!

Commercial banks make their money by the "spread" between the interest they pay to depositors (time and demand) and the rates they charge on loans. Well-managed banks may achieve a spread as high as three points, or roughly $30 per $1000 loaned. The secret of good banking is to confine loans to solvent borrowers so that few loans will have to be "written off" at a year end. Each new deposit expands the lending power of the bank, so there is a constant drive to attract new depositors. These are harder to get today because savings banks and S&Ls (who compete with commercial banks) are no longer limited to 5½ percent on passbook accounts, and can pay competitive rates. Further, many time accounts are now subject to check withdrawal, and commercial banks may pay 5¼ percent interest on average monthly checking balances above a certain minimum. Automatic tellers and computerized banking are also featured in today's competitive banking world, along with credit cards. Even with all these innovations, and intense competition, the best-run banks are splendid and growing moneymakers. Electronic banking and automatic tellers have led to the closing of marginal or losing branch offices. Bank America, for example, closed dozens of its smaller branches in California in 1983.

Deposits seem to be expanding fastest in the Sunbelt and Rocky Mountain states. In retirement areas, such as Florida and Arizona, there is a boom in trust business (for older and richer citizens), and the management of investment portfolios.

Banks seek to achieve a balance between commercial, real estate, agricultural, or consumer lending, but the composition of loan portfolios, in general, depends on the size of the institution and its location (rural, town, or metropolis), and the economic development in areas served. In Virginia there will be loans to tobacco farmers; in Iowa, to corn growers; in California, to vineyards; and in Texas, to oil drillers, etc.

Banks are able to expand their profits by virtue of high leverage, with about 5 percent in capital and surplus employed, and by drawing earning power from the other 95 percent of the bank assets as well. A large portion of each new deposit becomes automatically available for lending.

You may have observed that some of the most affluent individuals in your own community are substantial owners of bank shares (and frequently bank directors as well). A few years ago, a study of investments of a group of congressmen showed that, after real estate, bank stocks were the top choice among their equity holdings.

Historically, bank shares rank among the oldest common stocks in America. The Bank of New York (the first) was founded in 1784 and has paid dividends without interruption since 1785. Indeed, commercial banks have been indispensable to the development of our free-enterprise system. Often when towns were founded, especially in the Middle West, among the earliest establishments were the general store and a bank (and often a saloon!).

In the nineteenth century banks proliferated. The management of many was very slipshod and banks were grossly under-regulated. Banks could open their doors with only very limited capital, and virtually no professional financial management capability. They would take deposits, make loans, and many of them issued their own paper money, presumably backed by adequate gold reserves. This issuance and circulation of paper money proved especially popular because the currency would circulate for months or years from hand to hand in the community or beyond, and was seldom presented for redemption. The bank paid no interest on this paper money. It would make a loan, pay out the money to the borrower in its own paper dollars, and then collect interest on the loan.

Entrance to banking was uncomplicated and selling shares to open an institution, easily arranged. Farmers and traders could organize and operate a bank, but lending policies were sloppy and books seldom audited, so that state banks failed by the dozens during each "panic" in the nineteenth century. The national banks (under national charter) were, in general, stronger and they were regulated by the Comptroller of the Currency.

To stabilize the issuance of bank credit, to better assure the safety of bank deposits, and also to arrange for funds to be available in emergencies, the Federal Reserve System was organized in 1913. All national banks had to become members of "the Fed" and state banks, too, could join, if they applied and qualified. Members benefited from an orderly system for check collection, surveillance of reserves and loans, and auditing by their regional Federal Reserve Bank. (There are twelve such banks across the country.) More particularly, members could borrow from the Fed when necessary or desirable, at a special interest rate which has become known as the rediscount rate.

Most of the major metropolitan banks became members of the Federal Reserve (by buying stock in it), but there have always been thousands of state banks that have never joined. They did not like the requirement of keeping a percentage of their deposits in a special deposit at the Federal Reserve, and in general they "loaned out" a higher percentage of their deposits than did the Fed members.

However that may be, the Fed brought stability and better regulation to banking, but not enough to prevent hundreds of member banks from failing during the Great Depression.

Needed legislation has since notably improved banking practice; and, since 1934, depositors have had their funds insured in both state and national banks. The limit of deposit insurance protection on each account, originally $40,000, is now $100,000. People today do not worry so much about the solvency of their bank because they rely on the insurance protection provided by the Federal Deposit Insurance Corporation.

Even the FDIC, and strengthened auditing and supervision procedures introduced since 1933, have not eliminated bank failures. The United States Bank in San Diego, the Franklin National Bank in New York, the Penn Square Bank in Oklahoma City, the First National Bank of Midland, Texas, and, more recently, a cluster of banks in Tennessee, all failed. The procedure now, in cases of bank failure, is for the FDIC to pay off insured deposits or to find another and stronger bank to take over the troubled institution. This way there are no panicky withdrawals by worried depositors, and no long-term "freeze" of deposited funds.

Even in 1983 there were clouds in the banking sky—heavy write-offs on sour oil company loans by Continental Illinois and other banks—particularly in Oklahoma and Texas; and concern about the money center banks because of their massive credit extensions to Argentina, Brazil, Mexico, Venezuela, Nigeria, Poland, etc. While many loans to these financially extended nations are not actually in default, rolling over of maturities and delayed interest payments have occurred. Some nations have received new loans just to make interest payments on the old! The banking community does not seem to be worried, however, because large reserves have been set up, global economic conditions seem to be improving, and the International Monetary Fund has expanded the funds it has available for lending to countries with acute foreign-exchange problems.

Apart from the above qualifying factors, the commercial banks in the U.S. are flourishing, and in 1983 hundreds reported record deposits and earnings.

A sizeable number of bank stocks can qualify as Dowbeaters, and described below are a few selected for probable forward motion in the immediate future.

Bank of New York   BK   29¾

Multiple bank holding company.

BK's book value of $37.28 and continual growth record make it a foremost choice of blue-chip potential.

Barnett Banks of Florida   BBF   34½

A Florida bank holding company.

As Florida grows so grows BBF. Long-term growth of Florida will result in continual visits to the yearly new high list by BBF.

First Virginia Banks   FVB   16½

Banking.

We look for a continuation and an acceleration of FVB's growth in earnings, dividends, book value, and stock price in the years ahead.

Kentucky First National Corp   FKYN   30

Leading Kentucky bank holding company, and owning the First National Bank of Louisville. Annual increase in earnings for the past forty-one years. One percent return in assets and 15.2 percent earned on equity in 1982. There are 8,923,245 shares outstanding. Trades OTC.

NDB Bancorp. Inc.   NBD   40⅛

Banking.

This is another undervalued situation. An impressive and aggressive Detroit bank selling at 41, and 30 percent below book value of $61.93 per share. Indicated 1984 earnings of $7.15. Dividends, paid since 1935.

Norstar Bancorp.   NOR   31¼

Banking.

This New York state bank selling near book value of $30.15 is yielding more than 6 percent. A continuous record of consecutive earnings gains and a dividend history going back to 1804 puts NOR as a foremost Dowbeater bank stock selection.

Omaha National Corp.   OMAH   42½

Banking.

Here's another classy regional. It earned a net spread of 2.97 percent in 1982 and has a very broadly diversified loan portfolio. The stock should move from 42, increase its dividend, and possibly split within eighteen months.

Zion   NASDAO   30¼

Banking.

Zion is a major commercial bank in Utah. Zion also conducts consumer finance companies and industrial banks through twenty-eight offices in Utah, Colorado, Idaho, and Oregon. At 29, Zion stock sells at about seven times the 1983 earnings of $4.10.

9

For Whom
the Bell Toils*

This chapter is dedicated to the 3,200,000 stockholders in American Telephone & Telegraph as of December 31, 1983. They represented the largest group of share owners ever, in any corporation in the world. They were content with their investment because of its sustained investment quality and remarkable dividend record. Dividends on "T" (New York Stock Exchange trading symbol for the common stock) have been paid continuously since 1885, and for thirty-one years in a row (1920–51) at $9 a share. Through the years there were also two stock splits, and several valuable subscription rights.

At the end of 1983 T provided over 50 percent of the

*Some of the research material for this chapter was supplied by Market Alert, 18 Lois Street, Norwalk, Connecticut.

world's telephones, had assets of $155 billion, and 945 million shares of common stock outstanding, 75 percent owned by individuals. (The largest group was comprised of employees or retirees of AT&T.)

On January 1, 1984, however, all this was changed. After years of litigation by the U.S. Department of Justice, who sought to break up the company because they regarded it as too powerful a monopoly, there was a final agreement on January 8, 1982. This required AT&T to divest itself of all local telephone operations and of the publication and distribution of the *Yellow Pages*. The twenty-two operating Bell Telephone companies were to be regrouped and spun off into seven regional holding companies. Each new corporation was to have its own area of operation and management, issue its own debt and equity securities, arrange for public trading of its securities, and provide its own program for stockholder and public relations. Instead of reporting to Ma Bell, after January 1, 1984, each of these regional holding companies (RHCs) was to report to its own share owners.

The twenty-two Bell operating companies were realigned into the following RHCs: Bell South, NYNEX, Ameritech, Bell Atlantic, Pacific Telesis, Southwestern, and U.S. West. These seven RHCs jointly own a Central Staff Organization to continue the kinds of administration, engineering, and other technical services earlier provided by Ma Bell. All are now served by a computerized facility at Jacksonville, Florida, for stock transfers.

Each holding company provides local telephone service in its own area, with long-distance calls still handled by AT&T. These calls are now shared with competing independent telephone companies, including Sprint, MCI, and others.

The regionals retain the use of the Bell name (if desired), and *Yellow Page* directory publication service in their service area; also, ownership and operation of cellular phone systems, a share in new patent technology emanating from Bell Labs until 1989, and the right to market (but not to manufacture) customer premise equipment (phone sets, central switching systems, etc.).

The RHCs also have court approval to enter any new business, except the manufacture of telephone equipment and long-distance phone service. This permission is of special interest to investment analysts because it may stimulate regional managements to engage in data processing and computer operation, technological research into satellite and cable TV, telecomputing, mobile telephones, and other such ventures. Such operations might significantly expand the revenues and profits of innovatively managed companies and generate higher profit margins.

Naturally some of these regionals will be better managed, perform better, and develop new lines of business faster than others. All are faced with competition from such companies as Rolm, General Telephone, Mitel, MCI, General Electric, IT&T, and Webcor Electronics, to name a few.

In all of this drastic corporate transformation and transfer of assets facilities and services, what has become of the old AT&T? It carries on with its same stockholders and number of shares outstanding, but is a much diminished company as of January 1, 1984. While still providing 95 percent of domestic long-distance phone service, it has become more of a growth and technology company.

The streamlined AT&T, with $34 billion in assets, consists of Bell Laboratories (the research and development arm); AT&T Technologies (the manufacturing arm containing the factories and functions of Western Electric); AT&T Communications (the long-distance division); AT&T Information Systems (a separate facility set up to market nonregulated products and services); and AT&T International (the foreign marketing arm). There is also a real estate subsidiary, the computer company in Jacksonville, which handles all stock transfers for AT&T and the other seven companies. The Bell name (except for Bell Labs) and *Yellow Page* directories have been given over to the RHCs. The Western Electric brand name, however, has been retained by AT&T.

AT&T holds as investments 31.7 percent of the stock of Cincinnati Bell (worth $97.6 million on December 31, 1982), and 23.7 percent of Southern New England Telephone (worth $203 million at December 31, 1982). It plans, however, to divest itself of these holdings, and Cincinnati Bell has already arranged to buy back its stock.

The Effect of the Divestiture on Stockholders

The event, on January 1, 1984, was the most massive and significant corporate reorganization in history. Most people regarded it as costly and unnecessary, and wished that AT&T management had been more resolute in retaining its status as a nationwide regulated monopoly.

AT&T, under Ma Bell, provided the finest telephone service in the world, expanded to meet customers' needs, and kept its rates well below cost of living increases in other consumer sectors. Now it seems inevitable that phone rates will rise, service deteriorate, and investors will own shares in eight different companies instead of one. They will receive thirty-two dividend checks a year instead of four, if they retain the new shares distributed.

As a result of these structural changes, instead of owning one share of AT&T, as in the past, investors kept their AT&T stock and received one new share in each of the seven regional companies for each ten shares of T owned. Only whole shares were mailed out. Fractional shares were sold off and checks for the proceeds sent to the holders. Those holding fewer than ten shares of T received checks for fractions due.

In early 1984, at the time of delivery of new securities, there was considerable confusion among investors as to the best course of action. T stock, which had been selling (before the spinoff) at 63, dropped to 18. There was an indication that its 1984 dividend would be $1.20 (instead of $5.40). The retained shares yielded, on that basis, 6.5 percent instead of the 8.5 percent return on old shares. Shares in the new companies began to trade on the NYSE (when issued) on November 21, 1983 (although actual delivery was not made until February 16, 1984). Here's how the first day of "when issued" trading wound up.

NYSE Closing Prices 11/21/83

AT&T	18
Bell South	89
NYNEX	62¼
Bell Atlantic	70¼
Pacific Telesis	55⅛
U.S. West	59⅛
AmeriTech	65⅛
Southwestern	61⅝

Most investors, apparently, have retained all the shares they received. Many thousands, however, took advantage of AT&T's offer (until April 16, 1984), which permitted holders to buy or sell shares in any of the regionals for a commission of only 25 cents a share. This encouraged investors to consolidate their holdings by selling issues in one RHC and increasing holdings in one or more of the others. Investors seemed to favor the company that served their own home or office. Thus, stockholders residing in New York preferred to own NYNEX, while those in California opted for Pacific Telesis. It is still not at all clear in which of the new companies the stocks will be the best earners, or pay the highest dividends. But the group is so important a sector of the public utility industry that we thought it essential to make, in this book, some evaluation of the merits and potential of these offshoots of Ma Bell. We will start with the erstwhile parent (still among the most active stocks on NYSE)—the slimmed-down AT&T.

AT&T

The revised AT&T is a streamlined company moving forward from its traditional business—long-distance service and telephone equipment—into exciting, newly permissible areas.

AT&T Technologies, with $20 billion in assets, competes with other suppliers of telephone equipment (IT&T, Rohm, Northern Telecom, etc.) in carrying on Western Electric's traditional business with the operating companies. AT&T anticipates a substantial increase in foreign sales and places special emphasis on the continuing excellence of its research and development arm. Bell Labs pioneered in communications technology for years, acquiring over twenty thousand patents, including those for the computer, the laser, and dial phones. Half of its workers are now developing computer software, and, indeed, AT&T is scheduled to become a formidable competitor of IBM.

By 1943, Bell Labs had more patents and expertise in computers than anyone else, and might well have assumed the industry leadership but for a Justice Department ruling, in 1956, that AT&T could manufacture computers only for its own operations. The consent decree of January 1, 1984, changed all that. Now AT&T may legally sell software, computers, and services to anyone.

Accordingly, look for the rivalry to heat up between AT&T and IBM. AT&T computer plans are far-reaching—from small home models to large minicomputers, and all the network links between. AT&T has in place a line of #B computers. The large ones augment telephone switching, and the 3B20 model, with automation software, can send electronic mail and do screen editing. There are also minute desktop versions. Deals with Convergent Technologies and Olivetti (including a substantial stock ownership in that company) will accelerate T penetration of major computer markets.

There is also UNIX, an operating system to control voice and data communications; and PBX (private branch exchange) systems that can turn an office into its own miniature telephone company—plus a broad assortment of terminals.

All that needs to be demonstrated now is T's ability to merchandise this line of competitive products. It can sell, retail, through nine hundred stores already in place. AT&T

Information Services is expected to gross $2 billion a year from marketing telephone equipment and computerized services at unregulated prices.

In conclusion, T is almost a new company, and investors should regard its stock as a high-tech equity with gainful potentials from the current price of 16. (In March 1984 T sold off to below 16 when management expressed doubts about continuing the $1.20 dividend, which no longer made its primary attraction a high yield.) T is a growth stock and, after a little more seasoning, may move intelligently forward.

Here's the company projection for 1984:

Revenues	$56.6 billion	:	Assets	$34.7 billion
Net	$2.1 billion	:	Debt	$9.47 billion
Per share	$1.25 (est.)	:	Debt ratio	40 percent
Dividend	$1.20	:	Employees	385,000
	Shares outstanding	:	989.1 million	

The Regionals

It is difficult to rate the seven regional companies because we cannot, without a performance record, assess the capability of individual managements, or the extent to which traditional telephone business will be improved and expanded by technology and entries into new fields. More meaningful appraisals await the delivery of quarterly earnings reports and share-evaluations determined by the market place. We have, however, reviewed the material in the AT&T prospectus mailed to shareowners at the time of divestiture; and, from that data, present below our own current valuations.

Ameritech

Our first selection based on expectations of growth in earnings is Ameritech, the new name for the consolidated Bell group serving the Midwest: Illinois Bell, Indiana Bell, Michigan Bell, Ohio Bell, and Wisconsin Telephone. In 1982 Ameritech grossed $8.7 billion and earned $893 million in net income. Ameritech has the lead in cellular radio for mobile telephones, and there are 25 million auto registrations in its territory.

Efficiency of operations, minimal need for capital additions, and expanding cash flow point to enhanced earnings and dividends. There are 97,500,000 shares of Ameritech outstanding, with an indicated per-share net of $9.47 and a $6 dividend. The NYSE trading symbol is AIT.

U.S. West

Next on our list is U.S. West, which combines these former operating companies: Pacific Northwest, Mountain Bell, and Northwest Bell, serving a fourteen-state region, or 43 percent of the continental U.S. In 1982 the group had $16.3 billion in assets, revenue of $7.4 billion, and income of $837 million. The chairman, Jack MacAllister, notes that "U.S. West is not just a telephone company and might compete anywhere in any business." This "regional" was the first to organize for divestiture with a new name, board of directors, and a structured group of unregulated subsidiaries (for mobile phones, publishing, and equipment marketing).

Size, growth potential of the territory, and managerial clout should supply forward motion for U.S. West and create a superior total return in 1984. There are 98,000,000 shares of U.S. West outstanding, with estimated 1984 earnings of $8.96 per share, and a dividend of $5.40. The trading symbol is USW. In early March 1984 USW announced plans to buy in up to 2 million shares.

NYNEX

Third on our list is NYNEX, a blending of New York Telephone and New England Telephone, with combined assets of $18 billion in revenues and $973 million in net income (1982). NYNEX serves a seven-state region, with 10 million customers and a population of 30 million. The NYNEX neighborhood includes many of the most impressive names in industry, transportation, banking, insurance, real estate, recreation and higher education, and constitutes an intensively demanding market for sophisticated communication. A fine plant, leadership in fiber optics, and innovative management open broad horizons for NYNEX.

There are 98,300,000 shares of NYNEX outstanding, with estimated 1984 earnings of $9.84 per share, and a dividend of $6. The trading symbol is NYN.

Bell Atlantic

Fourth on our list is Bell Atlantic, which brings under one corporate roof Bell Telephone of Pennsylvania, New Jersey Bell, Diamond State Telephone (Delaware), and the Chesapeake and Potomac Companies.

Bell Atlantic had (at the 1982 year end) $17 million in assets, $8 billion in annual revenues, and $928 million in net income.

Technologically, Bell Atlantic is advanced, with 60 percent of all its customers served by electronic switching machines. The company is the leader of the seven in point of profitability.

Bell Atlantic rates well on the bases of area served, centrally controlled management, and growth potential.

The numbers for 1984: common shares, 98,300,000; earnings per share $9.69; and indicated dividend $6.40. The trading symbol is BEL.

Southwestern Bell

Next comes Southwestern Bell, which required no merger, but carries on the same business as before in the south-central section of the U.S. from Texas to Missouri. Southwestern Bell had assets of $17 billion and reached $851 million in net profits in 1982. The company has been among the leaders in lightwave lasers, microwave transmission, and high-speed digital switching systems.

Southwestern, serving five Sunbelt states, should benefit from regional growth. The 1984 estimates are: number of shares, 97,400,000; earnings per share, $8.93; and dividends, $5.60. The symbol is SBC, and the closing price, when issued on November 21, 1983, was 61⅝ to yield 9.09 percent.

Bell South Corporation

Bell South, a blending of Southern Bell and South Central Bell Telephone Companies, is the largest of the seven regionals, and probably the highest in investment quality. Assets (December 31, 1982) were $21.5 billion, revenues

$10 billion, and net income $1.3 billion. The company serves some 13 million customers in one of the fastest-growing regions in the nation. Bell South also led the group in profitability with a five-year average return on capital of 12 percent.

While we endorse Bell South as a quality leader, we feel its higher price inhibits its potential for capital gain. Others in the group will, we believe, attract a more animate market following.

Bell South has 98,200,000 shares outstanding, and expects to earn $12.21 in 1984 with a $7.80 dividend. The symbol is BLS and the first-day closing price was 89.

Pacific Telesis

Most analysts put this company at the bottom of the regional list because of its high debt ratio and its past rate problems with the California commission. The company has, however, a potential for a turnaround that may make it the speculative sleeper of the entire group.

Pactel is the combination of Pacific Telephone and Nevada Telephone. It serves the California-Nevada area and is historically the least profitable of the RHCs. It grossed $18 billion in 1982. Revenues reached $7.9 billion, and net profits, $63 million. Pactel has the highest debt ratio and lowest returns on invested capital in the group. It may be a sleeper, however, and benefit from improved rates and the vigor of the economy in the territory served. The shares closed at 55½ on November 21, 1983.

There are 98,100,000 shares of PAC outstanding, with indicated 1984 earnings of $8.00 and a dividend of $5.40.

In conclusion, we think T common is underrated below 16, and believe Ameritech, NYNEX and U.S. West may be the best performers among the regionals.

The New Bell Stocks
Suggested Profit Possibilities

		Symbol	Yield	PE
AT&T	15⅝	T	(7.62% yield)	7.8
Ameritech	66⅝	ATT	(9.01% yield)	7.0
Bell Atlantic	71⅜	BEL	(9.01% yield)	7.3
Bell South	93¾	BLS	(8.32% yield)	7.7
NYNEX	61½	NYN	(9.84% yield)	6.4
Pacific Telesis	57⅝	PAC	(9.4% yield)	7.1
Southwestern Bell	58⅝	SBC	(9.63% yield)	6.5
U.S. West	59⅜	USW	(9.11% yield)	6.6

◨◈

Dowbeater

Convertible Bonds

The high level of interest rates in recent years have greatly enhanced the attractiveness of that interesting hybrid security—the convertible bond. This type of obligation was introduced by the Southern Pacific Railroad in the late nineteenth century. Since then, it has become increasingly popular with investors because it uniquely combines the security and income dependability of a bond with the speculative zing of a common stock. It is a conservative way "to play the stock market" and offers many advantages to the corporate borrower as well.

A convertible bond is the unsecured long-term obligation of a corporation, assuring fixed, semi-annual interest payments. In addition, it can be exchanged, at the option of the

106

bondholder, for a specified number of shares of stock, usually of the issuing company.

In rare instances it can be converted into a preferred stock, or the shares of another company. General Cinema 10's of 2008, for example, can be exchanged for 15.9 shares of Reynolds Industries, Inc.

For the borrowing corporation, the advantages of marketing a new issue of "converts," rather than "straight" debentures, are important. If the debentures of the company would require, for example, a 13 percent coupon rate in order to attract buyers, the company could save a lot of money (in annual interest payments) by offering a convert whose rate could be 25 percent or 30 percent lower—possibly 10 percent instead of 13 percent. That is because converts are far more popular with investors. Because they are easier to sell, the investment firm will charge a lower underwriting commission, perhaps 3 percent or 4 percent instead of 6 percent.

Next, a corporation may select a convertible because, under favorable market conditions, the bond will, later on, redeem itself and convert from debt into equity. The common stock, then issued, will conserve corporate cash because the dividends on the new common shares will invariably total less than the interest payment on the bond.

The corporation will usually set the conversion rate (at the time of issuance) at 15 percent to 25 percent above the (then) prevailing market price of the common stock. If, for example, shares of XYZ Co. trade at 20, the specified conversion price may be 25. To state it differently, each $1000 bond would be exchangeable for 40 shares of XYZ common stock.

Also, a less sturdy corporation may issue a convertible bond at a time when its straight debenture could not be sold. It follows that converts may be employed by weaker, younger companies to raise needed capital (often to pay off bank loans); or by large, seasoned companies who, by offering converts, are really selling their common stock at a 20 percent premium.

Either type of company might successfully raise capital at a time when it could not sell common stock easily, or only at too low a price. During the period 1980–83, for example, many commercial banks sold convertible debentures because they did not wish to market their capital stocks at below book value. An instance of this is the Bank of New York 12's of 2006, convertible into 40 shares of common (now selling at 30).

Another corporate advantage in issuing converts is the "call" provision. Most debentures specify a call price, prior to maturity, at a 5 percent or even a 10 percent premium over par. In the case of XYZ Co. bonds, above, if the common stock rose to 40, then each $1000 bond would have a convertible value of $1600 (40 shares x $40). At that point the company might decide to call the bonds for redemption at 105 ($1050 per bond). Obviously the holders would not give up their bonds for $1050 when they were worth $1600. They would either sell or convert. In the end the company would "force" conversion, and (1) eliminate interest payments on the bonds, and (2) rub out the bond issue as a liability on its balance sheet.

Investors are cautioned that, at the time of public offering, a convertible debenture may be overpriced. By waiting, the bonds may, on occasion, be acquired below the issue price. Debentures issued years ago, when interest rates were far lower, often sell at discounts of 25 percent to 35 percent, and may merit investigation if the company has good prospects.

Even a forlorn convertible can be brought back to life. In 1976 Budd Co., a rather drab maker of railroad and transit cars, had a 5⅞ percent "bond" selling at $580. The bond was convertible into 45.23 shares of Budd common, which was then trading at around $11. In January 1978, however, a German firm offered to take over Budd at $36 a share, and the bonds became worth $1460 apiece on February 1, 1978. A handsome gain in less than two years!

Converts almost invariably sell at premiums over their convertible values because: (1) the yield is higher than that derived from the same sum invested in the common, and (2) downside risk is less than in holding common stock.

When shopping for convertible bonds, here's what you should look for:

1. A promising company whose common stock is currently undervalued and earnings are uptrending;
2. A low premium above the conversion price;
3. A sizeable active issue, preferably listed on the NYSE; and
4. A favorable stock market (your bond won't go up unless the stock does!).

You should also ascertain the number of shares into which the bond converts, or the price per share; the conversion value (i.e., the number of shares deliverable times the current price per share); the investment value, or what the bond would sell for on the market if it had no conversion feature. In general, don't buy the common stock of a company if it has a "close to market" convert. Buy the convert for higher yield, better downside protection, and stronger collateral value, if you're buying on margin. Almost all converts are "subordinated" debentures; that is, they are claims on the assets of a company, inferior to those of a straight debenture or a mortgage bond.

In describing converts we are not referring to a rare or obscure investment vehicle, but to a popular form of debt security that can be highly profitable in confident markets. Merrill Lynch 9½ percent debentures rose in 1982–83 from 104 to 237 (before they were called for redemption).

When you have chosen the issue of a strong company in a strong market, you can be a big winner. Buy around par, and think about selling when the bond passes 140. When it's time to move on, sell the bond and look for another equally good one at, or below, par. Don't convert! Convertible bonds provide plenty of action and profitability for informed traders.

There are several hundred issues from which to choose; and a number of mutual funds with excellent performance records that invest almost exclusively in converts. Converts are custom-built for conservative investors who are eager to participate in volatile markets. Comb the market for a list of bonds that interest you. Include discount issues, even some whose conversion potentials may appear remote. Discount bonds are, in the long run, moving up to par, and are unlikely to be called for early redemption.

We have, in the foregoing, made a fairly decent case for investing in convertible bonds. They insulate you from tragic losses, yet can generate rewarding capital gains. We think our Dowbeater goal of 30 percent a year in total return is a reasonable expectation, if you select intelligently in this sector. Be on the lookout for newcomers—either publicly underwritten, or emerging as a result of a corporate merger or reorganization. In general, converts that sell at a 50 percent or higher premium over conversion value are too remote, although one or two may come to life, as the Budd bonds did. Also, prefer bonds with large amounts outstanding, for active trading markets; and buy into aggressive companies where the common stock can supply some zing. Languid stocks deliver lean profits!

There are also some hybrids such as Sunshine Mining Co. 8½'s of 1995, which may be paid off either at $1000 or in 50 ounces of silver!

We have not referred here to a broad group (over 200 issues) of convertible preferred stocks, which are somewhat comparable. We have omitted them (though many provide good performance potentials) because we favor debt securities with fixed interest payments to equities with theoretically inferior income assurance. Moreover, convertible preferreds are heavily bought by corporations who get a tax credit of 85 percent on dividends received. This feature causes convertible shares to be heavily bought by cash-rich companies and priced to yield less than convertible bonds of comparable investment grade.

If preferreds interest you, however, we suggest that you investigate the data on: Anheuser Busch $3.60, UAL $2.40, Allied Corp. $6.74, Cigna $2.75, and Georgia Pacific $2.24.

In buying converts, we suggest that you invest in at least three issues, for diversification, and try to buy at or below par, and in the early stages of bull markets. It is not uncommon for converts to gain 30 or 40 points in a year.

Convertibles have the additional virtue of providing good investment returns while you wait for a resumption in a bull market. If you don't think the stock is promising, however, don't buy the converts. And be on the constant lookout for dynamic new issues.

Here are some attractive new issues now available (as of 3/10/84):

Dowbeater Convertible Bonds

Issue	Rate	Maturity	Bond Quotation	Shares per Bond	Conversion Price	Stock Quotation
Hospital Corp.	9	2008	94$\frac{1}{2}$	24.29	$ 41.17	37$\frac{3}{4}$
Bally Mfg.	10	2006	85$\frac{1}{4}$	30.6	32.70	15$\frac{7}{8}$
J. P. Stevens	9	2008	91$\frac{1}{2}$	33.05	30.25	21$\frac{3}{8}$
Trinity Indust.	7$\frac{7}{8}$	2008	91	28.50	27.00	21$\frac{1}{4}$
Sheller Globe	10	2006	97$\frac{1}{2}$	37.04	35.00	22$\frac{1}{4}$
La Quinta Motor Inns	10	2002	98	47.76	20.94	16$\frac{1}{4}$
Alaska Air	9	2003	99$\frac{1}{2}$	55.17	18.125	13$\frac{1}{2}$
Mapco	10	2005	87$\frac{1}{2}$	26.9	45.70	25$\frac{5}{8}$
Dreyfus Corp.	7$\frac{3}{8}$	2008	87$\frac{1}{2}$	13.5	74.00	26$\frac{1}{2}$
Boeing	8$\frac{7}{8}$	2006	115	23.7	42.20	41$\frac{1}{8}$
Hughes Tool	9$\frac{1}{2}$	2006	86	21.2	47.20	18$\frac{1}{4}$
Bank of N.Y.	12	2006	126	40.6	24.65	29$\frac{3}{4}$
Eastman Kodak	8$\frac{1}{4}$	2007	92$\frac{3}{4}$	9.9	102.30	67$\frac{3}{4}$

Bonds Convertible into Other Company Shares

Issue	Rate	Maturity	Bond Quotation	Shares per Bond	Conversion Price	Stock Quotation
General Cinema	10	2008	98 (Reynolds Industries)	15.9	$62.80	57¾
Internorth	10½	2008	98½ (Mobil Oil)	25	$40.00	31
Sun Oil	10¾	2006	94 (Becton Dickinson)	16.7	$59.90	34½

The above group is a representative shopping list of convertible bonds.

PART FOUR
DOWBEATER
SPECULATIONS

⊓⊓
Profits in
Takeovers

In a book designed to winnow out from the general run of stocks those able to outperform the DJIA and possibly double within two years, some attention should be paid to acquisition and mergers. Indeed, some of the most rapid and substantial capital gains in recent markets were in takeover stocks. A number of "target" issues advanced 75 to 100 percent in a matter of weeks, as bidding for them became hotly contested. Gulf Oil soared to $80 in 1983.

The classic case in 1977 was Babcock and Wilcox. In March 1977, this stock was minding its own business, modestly trading around $35. Out of the blue came United Technologies, with a takeover bid of $42. Then J. Ray McDermott & Co. got into the act and began buying shares in the open market. United Technologies raised the ante to $48. McDermott raised to $55 and finally to $65 a share to buy enough B & W shares to give it 49 percent. The B & W management had disfavored becoming part of United Technologies and had set up legal obstacles against UT, regarding McDermott as a more desirable and acceptable purchaser.

Stockholders in B & W made more money on their shares within a few weeks than they had for some years earlier. From $35 to $65 is almost 90 percent! Stockbrokers prospered on the deal, too, through heavy daily trading volume; and the investment bankers (and lawyers) who counseled the companies pocketed fees that made negotiated commission business look mousy!

This contest for ownership and control was no isolated phenomenon. Mergers and acquisitions in 1976 amounted to more than $20 million and aggregated close to $18 billion in 1977. The big year, however, was 1969, with a grand total of $24 billion involved. The takeover boom may now be slowing down a bit, perhaps because so many natural "quarries" have already been absorbed. We may expect many more mergers, but they will probably be fewer in number than currently, and involve bigger companies.

Before we arrive at specific ideas on where to look for merger stocks that may outperform the Dow it might be well to examine motivations. Why does a substantial corporation desire to buy out another for cash? Why is it willing to pay a premium over the historic price range, in which the target issue had been trading? Why not use that money to build a new plant, to improve or add to existing capital equipment? The best answer to those questions is that it's cheaper to buy than to build! Indeed, for many companies loaded with cash, a takeover may be one of the best investments it can make.

The identification of a takeover candidate usually starts with its financial statements. If these reveal a strong cash position, modern and well-maintained equipment, and a stock selling at a low multiple and well below its book value, then a company becomes attractive. A record of stable and preferably rising earnings and sales is also desirable.

The company under consideration may fit in well with the acquisitor's main line of business (as when International Nickel absorbed ESB, a maker of storage batteries, or Pepsico took over Pizza Hut). The target may have a stodgy and tired management so that injection of a new executive team might dramatically improve its earning power. Sometimes the motivation is either to diversify or flatten out the cyclical nature of the acquisitor's business, or to provide entry into an entirely new field. The latter was the case when Mobil took over Marcor. Moving into a new industrial sector may also seem desirable if a traditional business is phasing out, or operating at steadily declining profit margins.

The name of the game is to earn profit, whether in your own line or someone else's. If the target corporation's shares sell below "book," and the company is earning 10 to 12 percent on invested capital and growing at a rate of 8 to 10 percent annually, it becomes worth considering. In general, the buyer wants to purchase below stockholders' equity because it must write off any price excess over book value (good will) over a period of no longer than forty years. Any such "write-off" reduces reported profits.

Companies that make takeovers today seem willing to pay, on the average, 60 to 70 percent higher than earlier quotations for a stock (1) to be sure they get the company, (2) to shake out reluctant sellers, (3) to get their hands on a cash-rich balance sheet, (4) because book value may be grossly understated and the properties of the target company could not now be duplicated for double or treble their depreciated values, (5) to get a "hot" management team or instant penetration of a desired market. If a company decides to enter the convenience-food industry, for example, it can do so more economically by buying a company already entrenched in that field than by starting from scratch.

Just because there have been so many mergers and there's a headline on the financial page about a new one almost daily does not mean they are easy to complete. No, indeed. First, the target company may not want to be acquired (most don't). It may defend by hiring attorneys, getting friends and employees to buy more stock, employing an investment house as consultant, soliciting proxies, and advertising in the financial press. Also, there are now anti-takeover laws in thirty-one states that may impede or block a merger. A reluctant company may also invoke antitrust laws or call upon regulatory agencies such as the SEC to intervene. Such tactics as these may delay a merger or impose so many roadblocks and legal and accounting expenses that "the wolf" will go away.

Finally a company, helpless against invasion, may look around to find a friendlier wolf. When Occidental Petroleum sought to take over Kern County Land a few years back, the Kern management was unhappy at the prospect of being run by Occidental. Within weeks a newfound brother, Tenneco, Inc., was approached and persuaded to take over Kern. Occidental lost out, but did make a few millions in capital gains on the sale of the Kern stock it had purchased along the way.

Incidentally, it is almost standard operating procedure for an acquiring company to buy a chunk of target stock (maybe 5 or 10 percent) before trundling out its big guns.

It has become an important divisional operation of several big Wall Street firms to search for takeover candidates, to structure strategic mergers, and to help find new suitors if the first one is disliked; and to calculate the offering prices most likely to win properties and to "keep out the grocery clerks." The majors in this field would include Morgan Stanley & Co., Goldman Sachs & Co., Kidder Peabody, Solomon Bros., Lazard Freres, Lehman Brothers, First Boston, and White Weld, etc.

As long as the prices of common stocks remain relatively low and with prevailing P/E multiples of 9 or 10 (preferably lower), and so long as there are dozens of publicly held companies around with earning assets very costly to replace (but reasonably priced for acquisition) and big companies with plenty of surplus cash, you'll continue to see a parade of merger proposals. (Where no other companies appear that are attractive, the next best thing to do seems to be to buy in your own stock, as IBM, Tandy, Teledyne, Mite Corp., etc., have done.)

Recent acquisitions were impressive: General Electric took over Utah International; Unilever bought National Starch & Chemical; Arco won Anaconda Copper; International Tel. and Tel. acquired Eason and Carbon Industries; Kennecott offered what seemed a gaudy price ($66 a share) for Carborundum; Allegheny Ludlum took Chemetron; Union Carbide added Amchen Products; Nestlé Products (Switzerland) acquired Alcon Laboratories; Standard of California took over Gulf at $80; Royal Dutch offered $58 for Shell Oil; Texaco paid $45 for Superior Oil. Takeover bids don't always prevail, however. In 1977 Sambos Restaurant, Koehring, Western Publishing, and Applied Digital Data were all wooed. Their stocks bounced up on the rumors, but no takeovers occurred. Quaker State bought in its own stock at $24 to avoid takeover.

Somewhat related to takeovers is this phenomenon—a company buying its own shares in the open market or making a tender offer. This, too, is of interest to investors in quest of capital gains. When a company has developed a rich cash flow and strong current balance-sheet position, and decides not to make acquisitions, it may choose to spend some of its surplus funds buying in its own stock. The classic examples of this are IBM, which laid out $700 million to buy its shares at $280, and Teledyne, which paid $200 each for 8.7 million shares.

Why should a company buy its stock, engaging in what Wall Street calls "corporate cannibalism?" There are several pretty plausible reasons:

1. To reduce the number of outstanding shares and by so doing increase the earnings and dividends per share accruing to the remaining equity.
2. To satisfy stockholders who may have complained that their shares weren't getting sponsorship.
3. To provide a measure of market support in the issue when general interest in it is lagging.
4. To express confidence in the desirability of its own shares.
5. To have treasury shares available for pension, or bonus plans, or to be offered in a desired merger.
6. To buy in at a low multiple. If a company buys in stock at five times earnings, it is making 20 percent on its money.

The objections to the practice are that (1) growing companies should be seeking more stockholders and wider distribution of shares rather than contracting the amount of

stock in public hands; (2) larger cash dividends on outstanding stock would please shareowners and motivate market
action better; (3) a well-managed company should use its
cash to expand earning assets, enter new product lines, and
engage in forward-looking research rather than limit or
reduce the scope of its operations.

In actual practice, we are not aware of instances where a
company's announcement of a stock repurchase has zoomed
its shares, although it may have prevented them from declining further. In any event a takeover rumor or announcement is far more likely to produce a swift capital gain for
you than a program of treasury stock buying.

From the foregoing, we conclude that there exist quite
frequently opportunities for short-run capital gains stem-
ming from takeover talk or rumors to firm cash bids for
particular issues. Once mentioned, a stock that might have
been languishing for months at a so-so price begins to attract
a following, and previous valuations of the issue are revised
upward in light of its newly found "merger bait" characteristics. Volume in the issue expands and traders have no dif-
ficulty moving in and out, on attractive interim swings.

If you acquire shares of the target company as soon as
the rumor surfaces, your chances of gain become excellent
and chances of loss minimal. The subject stock is almost
certain to enter a new and higher market orbit. Among the
best performers of 1977 were takeover candidates such as
Carborundum, American Medicorp, Miles Laboratories, National Starch & Chemical and, more recently, Sun Oil,
Disney Corp., City Investing, and Shell Oil.

To illustrate the importance of early entry into a merger
situation, observe the market action in two representative
instances. Miles Laboratories hadn't shown much animation

and was trading at $25 when management announced that merger discussions were in progress. That release was sufficient to push the shares up to $29. Next the buyer, Bayer A.G., a major German industrial company, announced it would pay up to $40 a share, and when shareowners were languid in their response, increased the offer to $47, ultimately the winning price.

Alcon Laboratories was selling at 25 when a large Swiss buyer, Nestlé S.A., surfaced and later announced a tender offer at $42, which on November 21, 1977 propelled the shares to 41⅝. In both of these cases, investors were shown a fairly clear highway to rewarding profits. Even when takeover announcements do not materialize, the target stocks usually behave reasonably well, and make money for those who bought on the first press release. Merger bait shares generally sell in higher price ranges, even after a takeover bid that didn't jell.

If there are competitors, instead of just one buyer on the horizon, so much the better. American Medicorp, like the Babcock & Wilcox case, illustrates the benefits of competitive striving. Humana, another hospital company, was all set to take over American Medicorp at around $15 a share in stock, when TWA, with its Hilton International subsidiary, came up with a better offer, $20 a share in cash. AM rose in 1977 from $8 to $21¼, a gain of 165 percent.

Merger negotiations place special obligations on corporate officers and directors. First, they must publicly disclose the possibility of takeover as promptly as possible, lest stockholders sell stock in ignorance and sue management for profits lost due to nondisclosure of important information. Second, officers are not supposed to benefit from "inside information." For example, they may not, in good conscience, buy more of their own stock on the strength of an attractive merger bid in the offing. Equally, the management of the acquiring company is expected (1) to publicly announce its intentions as promptly as possible, (2) to inform its own stockholders, and (3) not to buy stock in the target company in the knowledge that a higher price will ultimately be paid for it. This is the age of stockholder suits and class actions, so officials must be honorable and discreet, if only to avoid lawsuits!

While most recent takeovers have been for cash, the tax-free exchange of securities is still desirable in many cases, although wide swings in the prices of the stocks involved may cause exchange offers to be modified or withdrawn. Also some acquirers have grown impatient with managements that drag their feet in accepting a cash offer, and have on occasion reduced the tender price, or threatened to do so, to accelerate a decision. This may also place blame on officers and directors for their failure to accept or act upon an attractive offer, and might lead to a stockholders' suit, if the final offer were less than a rejected earlier offer.

In any event, it is decidedly worthwhile for investors to keep alert to possible mergers because the gains for early birds can be swift and substantial, and the risks of loss quite low. As soon as you read about a possible buyout on the financial pages, or see it announced on a news ticker, investigate. If the company sought has a good earning record for three prior years, a sound balance sheet, well-regarded products or services, if its stock is thinly held by management, and if management has appeared inept and unimaginative, the company will probably be snapped up, and you'd better get aboard. If a big, well-run company such as City Investing is up for grabs, the acquirer has to be a strong, well-heeled company, and the profits from early purchase of the quarry shares seem well assured. The only people who are willing to pay well "over market" for stocks recently are expanding companies—or Arabs! The buyers today are much stronger than the conglomerate traders of the 1960s, and they are building sturdier corporate clusters and stronger capitalizations.

Suggested Takeover Possibilities

City Investing	ANV	35½
Crane	CR	32⅞
Disney	DIS	63⅞
Gulf Broadcasting	GBCO	8⅛
Mesa Offshore Trust	MOS	2⅝
Noble Affiliates	NBL	17½
Northwest Industries	NWT	46¾
Occidental Petroleum	OXY	28⅝
Storer Broadcasting	SCI	32½
Unocal	UCL	35½

One clue you can get to possible takeover is an existing minority investment. Many of the companies listed above are already partially owned by possible acquirers.

Watch these and many others and you may cash in on the merger. Always buy the takeover stock, not that of the wolf!

12

Precious Metals
as Dowbeaters

Our book would not be complete without coverage of precious metals because, in the last twenty years, some of the most dramatic speculative gains have been recorded among gold and silver shares. Within this period, gold has zoomed from $35 an ounce to $850; and silver, from $1.29 an ounce to $48.80. (Both highs were registered in January 1980).

These great swings in gold and silver resulted from inflation, combined with the spectacular trading of the Hunt family in 1980. As of April 1984, inflation appeared to be under control; but many economists are predicting its return due to our huge national deficits and the substantial increase in the money supply of 1983–4. Accordingly, investors should be prepared and plan to allocate some of their funds to gold and silver shares. The increasing industrial demand for both metals, together with the possibility of a return of inflation, justify such a program.

Gold

For over six thousand years, gold has been man's most cherished portable asset. Around 4000 B.C. Egyptian farmers, drawing water from the Nile, were fascinated by the grains of yellow metal they saw glistening in the shallow water near the river bank. What they saw was gold, and it immediately became a prized possession.

Gold is virtually indestructible. It is malleable, lustrous, and ornamental. It is heat-resistant, a conductor of electricity, has unique insulating qualities, and is readily alloyed with other metals.

The glitter of gold has proved eternally attractive. Its beauty was embodied in personal adornments, which became the envied symbols of status, wealth, and power in early societies. Gradually the mining, and possession, of gold became royal or government prerogatives. First extracted from the beds, terraces, and deltas of rivers—the Nile, the Euphrates, the Oxus (flowing into the Black Sea), and the Pactolus (in Asia Minor)—alluvial gold was easy to mine. Gold was later sought below ground by means of adits, tunnels, and shafts. Gold was mined in Greece and Spain; and the gold stores located in Mexico and Peru in the 1600s transformed world history. Later came the great strikes of gold in California, the Klondike, Canada, and in South Africa—the richest mines in the world today.

What introduced gold into the world economy was the coinage of money. Early trade was conducted by barter. What was needed, however, was something to serve as a medium of exchange, a store and standard of value, and a unit of accounting. Gold filled the bill, and was first used as currency in crude bars or rings. Later, rings of nearly uniform weight were made. The breakthrough occurred in 550 B.C. when King Croesus of Lydia invented coinage. He struck coins of gold and silver, crude objects shaped like lima beans. The use of coins in commerce and trade caught on rapidly, and gold became the standard monetary metal of the world. Between 1821 and 1904 most of the modern nations went on a gold standard. They used paper money (which was invented around 1700), but backed by, or convertible into, gold coins. The price of gold during most of the nineteenth century was stabilized at $20.47 an ounce.

Even with all the mines that have been excavated over the years, gold is still a very scarce metal. All the gold aboveground in the world (93,000 metric tons), could easily be stowed on the Queen Elizabeth. Indeed, 90 percent of all the gold ever mined is still in use. About 40 percent of the world's gold is held by central banks—the largest holding is 264 million ounces, by the Unted States.

The gold standard died on August 15, 1971, when President Nixon closed the gold window, and the U.S. Treasury ceased to buy or sell gold at $35 an ounce. A world trading market developed. The price rose from the former official figure of $35 an ounce (maintained from 1934–1971) to a giddy high of $850 an ounce in 1980. It is $390 an ounce today, and on its way back up. Gold and silver are both desirable metals to own in this phase of our economy, if only as hedges.

Silver

Silver was found in Egypt and Mesopotamia some six thousand years ago and early became highly valued for its own special qualities. Silver possesses a unique, moonlike luster and is among the most enduring of metals. Following gold into coinage, widely circulated silver coins included the drachma of Greece, the denarius of Rome, the rupee of India, the tael of China, the thaler of Austria, the shilling of England, and U.S. silver coins from a dime to a dollar. But like gold, silver has become too valuable to be used in coins. The last 90 percent U.S. silver coins were struck in 1965. Since then the silver content of half-dollars was reduced and other coins are now of clad metal—copper and zinc. Silver, which sold at $1.29 an ounce in 1965, soared to $48.80 in 1980. Today it is $9.00 an ounce and several respected economists predict a return to above $25. Judicious investment in silver is therefore recommended.

Silver remains scarce. In the free world 265 million ounces of new silver were produced (in 1982) against world consumption (for coinage, photography, industry, jewelry, electronics, dentistry) of 369 million ounces. The shortage (over 100 million ounces) was made up from salvage from scrap, melted coinage, release from hoarding, and silver exports from India and Pakistan.

Silver is ten times as plentiful as gold in Nature, but still scarce. Silver occurs in two particular geological formations: shallow deposits uncombined with other metals; and affinity deposits where silver occurs in a mixture of metals, with copper, lead, zinc, nickel, cobalt, or gold, or combinations of these. The richest deposits have usually occurred within a few hundred feet of the surface and lent themselves to mining by open pit, rather than by shaft or tunnel. Most such are now exhausted.

Today the countries leading in the production of silver are Canada, Mexico, Peru, and the U.S. Russian production is estimated at about 50 million ounces a year, so that Russia is, on balance, an importer. So is China.

With these background sketches, we are now ready to approach investments in this area. In both gold and silver you can own the metal outright in bars, from fractions of an ounce to 1000 ounces or more. There are also millions of coins in both gold and silver that have been minted over the centuries. Some very scarce gold coins may bring $200,000 or more. Rare coin collectors generally prefer French Napoleons, English sovereigns, Dutch guilders, Venetian ducats, and the $5, $10, and $20 U.S. gold pieces minted since 1795. The so-called bullion (not scarce) coins include Krugerrands and Maple Leafs (each one ounce of gold) and the Mexican centenario, weighing a little over an ounce.

People collect silver half-dollars and dollars (especially the Morgan dollar); and bags of pre-1966 silver coins containing $1000 face amount (usually quarters or halves). These sell today for over $8000 each, and have been much higher.

You can also buy gold and silver futures on the commodity exchanges—contracts for future delivery for 100 ounces of gold, or for 1000 or 5000 ounces of silver. These contracts can be bought on margins as low as $3000, but they are risky, and we do not recommend the purchase of any commodity on margin.

Our province is marketable securities with gainful potentials; and we have researched a series of gold and silver stocks of definite promise.

Gold Stocks

The leading North American gold issue is Homestake Mining, listed on the NYSE and a barometer of the gold market. It is the largest American producer, turning out 260,000 ounces in 1983 in the U.S. plus 50,000 in Australia. HM has 37,195,000 shares outstanding, which earned $1.08 per share in 1983. When the gold market is moving, this is the most sensitive stock. HM is also a substantial producer of silver, lead, and zinc.

Another excellent gold share is a hybrid, Freeport Mc-Moran Inc., a major producer of sulphur, copper, and petroleum. It also has 70 percent ownership of Freeport Gold, which surfaced 186,000 ounces of gold in 1983. Freeport's earnings from gold alone were $23.3 million.

In 1983 FMI (NYSE symbol for common stock) grossed $786 million and earned $93 million or $1.32 per share, versus 95 cents in 1982. FMI is a diversified natural resource company and, in 1985, may become the leading U.S. gold producer (ahead of Homestake).

Stan West Mining Corp., an ably managed exploration company, is bringing back into production a series of formerly producing mines and adjoining properties in the Prescott-Jerome area of Arizona. Over 500,000 tons of proven resources have been defined, with an average assay of .3902 per ton. A 300-ton mill should be completed in early 1985 and the Stan West should become a low-cost producer. Stan West has about 10 million shares outstanding, and it trades on the OTC at 4.

American Gold

Other American goldstocks of merit would include Pegasus (12) with 6.2 million shares outstanding, and indicated 1984 production of 70,000 ounces; also Sonora Gold Corp.

in California (100,000 ounces) scheduled to go public as this was written. Inca Resources (4⅝) is scheduled for production of 50,000 ounces in 1985. Klondex (1½) is a small Nevada producer.

As the price of gold advances, look for many new mining issues to go public. But be careful! A high percentage will be losers—companies either running out of money, or ore—or both! Only one gold-mining company in 200 actually enters production.

Canadian Gold

Canada is, next to South Africa, the world's largest gold producer—surfacing over 2 million ounces annually. Mining there is on an uptrend, with new mines such as those in the Northwest Territories, and a series of major discoveries at Hemlo, Ontario, led by Lac Minerals.

Canadian Mines

Canadian mines are favored by investors because of the country's secure political and financial climate, and the active trading markets on exchanges in Canada and the U.S.

Our lead Canadian suggestion is Agnico-Eagle Mines Ltd., a low-cost producer with a very strong balance sheet and no debt; and indicated production of 72,500 ounces of gold in 1984 plus over 1 million ounces of silver. Agnico-Eagle is a long-life mining company that also owns 650,129 shares of Dumagami Mines, Ltd. and interests in Kiena Mines and Sudbury Contact Mines.

Agnico-Eagle earned 42 cents a share on 14,143,727 shares in 1983. Shares trade on Toronto Exchange and OTC in the U.S. (13½) under the symbol AEAGF.

Campbell Red Lake

The leading producer in Canada and the richest gold mine in North America is Campbell Red Lake Mines Ltd. It has the highest grade ore and lowest cost (Ca. $120 an ounce in 1983). Production in 1983 was 230,000 ounces. Proven reserves (1982 year end) were 2.04 million tons, grading .622 ounces to the ton. A new property at Detour Lake is expected to expand from 2750 tons per day capacity to 4000 tons per day and be developed as a deep mine at a total cost of Ca. $110 million. The company also has oil and gas interests, including stock in Dome Petroleum.

With current assets of Ca. $51.8 million and a long-term debt of only $12.5 million, CRK is financially strong. There are 47,994,000 shares outstanding listed on Toronto and on the NYSE (trading symbol CRK). Each share earned 80 cents in 1980 with a 38-cent dividend on each share.

Dowbeater List of Canadian Golds

Company	U.S. 2/14/84 Share Price	Estimated 1984 Gold Production	# Shares Outstanding
Little Long Lac	30¼	80,000	3.2 million
Echo Bay Mines	8	140,000	31.4 million
Kiena Mines	24	65,000	5.9 million
Agnico-Eagle	13½	72,500	14.1 million
Lac Minerals	26½	255,000	29.5 million
Dome Mines	14½	330,000	70 million
Campbell Red Lake	27¾	260,000	48 million
Int'l Corona Resources	9¾	50,000 (in 1985)	12.5 million

Of these, Little Long Lac, Lac Minerals, and International Corona have important holdings in the Hemlo, Ontario, district, where gold is found not in quartz veins, but in volcanogenic sediments. The Hemlo district may prove sensational.

South African Gold

South Africa is the world's largest gold-mining nation, responsible for about 70 percent of annual free world production. The mines there are located in the broad area spreading over several hundred square miles around Johannesburg. Several of the mines represent an investment of $150 million dollars or more.

The South African ore is a rich gravel-like conglomerate, averaging over 20 ounces to the ton, and appearing almost limitless. It is uniquely profitable to mine because the ore remains rich to great depths.

South African Gold Shares

President Steyn Gold Mining Co., Ltd. is one we favor. It is one of the best mines, with 14.6 million shares outstanding and low-cost production. President Steyn handles 400,000 tons of ore a year, with a $230 cost per ounce. We expect higher dividends in 1984–5.

Vaal Reefs Exploration and Mining Co., Ltd. is the largest gold mine in the world, producing over 2 million ounces annually. Relatively low cost $180 an ounce in 1983, a terrific earner and a long-life mine.

Other fine mines include Consolidated Dreifontein, the second largest; Western Deep Levels, a high-yielding stock, and Elanstrand, a lower-priced developing mine.

For across-the-board investment we like ASA Ltd., a closed-end investment company listed on the NYSE (Symbol ASA). Over 75 percent of its portfolio is in a screened group of South African golds. These shares provide excellent representation in gold and respond sensitively to market motion in the metal.

South African shares are valued because many of the mines have rich, long-life ore bodies and because they pay high dividends—often returning 10 to 15 percent on the cost of shares. They are traded on exchanges in Johannesburg, London, and Amsterdam; and on the OTC in the U.S. in the form of American Depository Receipts. Here's a representative group of equities we favor:

Selected South African Golds

Company	2/22/84 Share Price (U.S.)	Life of Mine	Per Share Estimated 1984 Dividends ($)
Consolidated Driefontein	35⅞	50 yrs.	$2.40
President Brand	43½	20 yrs.	$3.75
Southvaal	63½	30 yrs.	$3.00
Blyvooruitzicht	14¼	10 yrs.	$2.00
Stilfontein	16¾	13 yrs.	$2.20
ASA Ltd.	59	(investment trust)	$3.00
Vaal Reefs	131	30 yrs.	$7.50

Silver Stocks

Experts in precious metals believe that, because of rising industrial demands (particularly in electronics, computers, photography, and in China's expanding industrial economy) silver will advance more rapidly than gold. For centuries silver sold at a 16-to-1 ratio with gold. That ratio is now 32; and silver is the "lag" metal.

Over 75 percent of all silver produced comes as a by-product of mining other metals. Hence Asarco, a leading producer of copper and lead, is also the top U.S. silver producer.

Asarco is the first stock to discuss because of its global production of silver—over 11 million ounces of its own production annually, plus a 34 percent interest in a big Mexican company; a 52.3 percent interest in a Peruvian company; and a 44 percent interest in M.I.M. Holdings Ltd., a major Australian mining company.

Altogether, ASARCO accounts for over 18 million ounces of silver annually, and is, as well, a major producer of copper, lead, and zinc with extensive smelting and refining facilities. Its new Troy mine in Montana (opened in 1981) produces 4.5 million ounces of silver a year.

There are 28,254,000 shares of AR listed on the NYSE (30¾), which earned $1.54 in 1983. Higher earnings and quotations are indicated for 1984–5.

While ASARCO is mainly a by-product producer of silver, Hecla Mining (HL on the NYSE) is an almost pure silver producer. Its Lucky Friday mine in Idaho is a fine producer; and it also owns a 12½ percent interest in the Galena Mine and 5 percent of Coeur d'Alene. As this was written, Hecla planned to take over Ranchers Exploration by exchange of stock (1.55 shares of Hecla for one of Ranchers). When this is complete, Hecla will have an annual production of over 8 million ounces.

Before the merger offer, HL had 18,832,000 shares outstanding selling at 21, earning $1.05 a share in 1983. HL is the number-one stock to own as silver starts to move.

Coeur d'Alene Mines Corporation is another stock of merit in the Idaho sectors. Coeur d'Alene produces about 3 million ounces annually. There are 7,116,000 shares outstanding trading OTC under the symbol COUR (19). ASARCO, Hecla, and Callahan are all substantial stockholders. The common stock earned 52 cents a share in 1983. Coeur d'Alene is a rich, long-life mine. COUR also owns 49 percent of Royal Apex, a smaller mine, now coming into production.

The Callahan Mining group (CMN on the NYSE) is another representative silver mine, with 6,476,000 shares outstanding (22). CMN owns 50 percent of the Galena mine operated by ASARCO; and a one-twelfth interest in Coeur d'Alene. Callahan earned 48 cents in 1983 but should improve in 1984.

We are less impressed with Sunshine Mining because of its heavy capitalization. Its shares are listed on the NYSE (SSC), and it has an unusual 8½ percent bond issue outstanding, payable at maturity at $1000 or 50 ounces of silver.

Other American silver shares would include Phelps Dodge, a major producer of copper with heavy by-production in silver; and Homestake, the gold leader, is also significant in silver.

Canadian Silver Mines

Canadian silver mines are almost all by-product ones, so that less opportunity for direct investment in silver is available.

Among Canadians, the largest is Noranda—big in copper, lead, molybdenum, gold, and silver. Noranda has been hard-hit by low copper prices but could turn around. It handles over 15 million ounces of silver through its refineries, and is a huge company with 117,542,000 shares outstanding, trading on the Toronto S.E. (symbol NOR).

Agnico-Eagle, which we cited as a gold producer, will produce over 1 million ounces of silver in 1984 and is thus a dual investment in precious metals.

Other by-product producers include Cominco Ltd., a subsidiary of Canadian Pacific—important in lead, zinc, copper, and chemicals. Cominco mines around 9 million ounces of by-product silver. Tech Corp., Falconbridge Copper, Hudson Bay Mining, and Brunswick are also in silver.

United Keno was a rich mine, but ran out of ore. Echo Bay is a gold producer and surfaces a million ounces of silver a year, as well.

A company we favor is Lacana Mining Corporation, a Canadian company with its principal properties and earning assets in Mexico. Lacana has a 30 percent interest in the Torres mine in Guanajuato, Mexico, and the Encantada Mine. These mines produce about 7 million ounces annually, from rich pure silver mines in production for over four hundred years. Lacana also has interests in two excellent gold mines in Nevada.

Lacana has 10,915,000 shares outstanding, trading on the Toronto S.E. and OTC in the U.S. under the symbol LCNAF.

Another Mexican producer is Fresnillo; and in 1983 the Real de Angeles mine opened—the largest open-pit silver mine in the world—producing at a rate of 7.5 million ounces a year.

Improving mines are Candelaria Mines in Nevada, Sixteen-to-One in Silver Peak, Nevada, and the Escalante Mine in Utah.

As you consider silver mines, look for good grades of long-life ore (preferably 15 ounces to the ton or better), the number of shares outstanding, and the capability of management.

Gold and silver have been choice investments for centuries. They are in line for another price explosion in the years immediately ahead. Several of the shares we listed will be stellar Dowbeaters.

13

Lazarus Securities:
Stocks to Come Up
from the Dead

The trouble with Wall Street in recent years is that most of the zest and adventure have been removed. Today's "players" seem meekly content to lodge most of their surplus funds in 12 percent bonds, mutual funds of all descriptions, traditional common stocks for fixed income, balanced funds, municipal bonds, growth and energy, etc. These may all be reasonably prudent vehicles for the deployment of money, but most are geared primarily to safety of principal and comfortable yields. They are quite devoid of any speculative zing or possibility of exciting expectation of gain in market prices.

With 70 percent of all transactions on the Big Board now executed for institutional accounts, and with pension and welfare funds totaling over $500 billion, the portfolio accent is heavily on large, seasoned companies with millions of outstanding listed shares. Probably at no time in Wall Street history has there been so little effort expended in an eager quest for high-percentage capital gains.

Toward that objective, this chapter examines a sector of the market that is the native habitat of shares generating the most explosive market action. These lower-priced issues can move up and down with pace and animation, and since 1968 they have been woefully neglected by brokerage firms and investors. People with market funds seem to have lost their sporting blood. Why? Because of the solemn institutionalization of investment procedures; because of significant structural changes that have taken place within the securities business; and finally because, since 1968, speculators in general have not made out very well, and market "killings" have been few and far between.

Consider the changes in the machinery of Wall Street within the past decade. Firms have disappeared in droves. Many formerly well-known NYSE brokerage houses have gone out of business or have merged for survival purposes. Those firms that remain have contracted their sales forces and notably reduced their research departments. Thus, today the number of security issues regularly "covered" by exchange firms has greatly contracted, and the stress, in both research and sales, is heavily on seasoned blue chips and traditional "glamour" issues; or on companies with which the larger firms maintain continuing investment banking relationships.

Consequently, thousands of substantial companies with publicly traded shares are not being researched or recommended at all by brokerage houses. Reports or market letters are now rarely prepared or distributed on them (except by the investment advisory services), and smaller, early phase companies with low-priced inactive issues get no notice at all. This situation is further aggravated by the departure of hundreds of small broker/dealer firms that entered the business in the 1960s, primarily to underwrite new issues. When the fad was over, they disappeared from view. As a result, hundreds of smaller secondary companies that went public in that era have no market sponsorship today. Stocks are like any other consumer goods; you have to know about them before you will buy them. Today, nobody is telling the story of these second-or third-tier publicly owned corporations.

Not only are earlier underwritings of fledgling enterprises languishing and neglected in the over-the-counter market, but there is almost no activity in the origination and distribution of new issues. In 1969, more than 1000 new issues were publicly offered; in 1977, fewer than thirty of any substance (not counting Regulation As and small local mining and corporate promotions). There is a strong comeback in new issue underwriting in 1984.

These stocks, however, are far and away the best bet for the small speculator—someone who has perhaps only $500 to $1000 to invest.

In addition to the general absence of dissemination of information about thousands of lesser-known or regional companies, there is an adverse attitude toward doing business in the lower-priced shares of second-or third-tier corporations, whose shares trade inactively. Roadblocks are set up by major brokerage firms, and thus they may:

1. Decline to accept or execute an unsolicited buy order on a stock selling below $5.
2. Request a statement by the customer that he or she is

buying the stock "on his own" and not on the basis of any recommendation, expressed or implied, by the firm.

3. Ban the solicitation by customers' brokers of orders in "below $5" issues or deny commission credit on any such orders, if taken and executed.

4. Execute orders in low-priced OTC stocks only "at the market" and not at a specified price.

5. Maintain a policy that "our brokers will attempt to dissuade clients from buying low-priced or unseasoned stock"; and to warn clients about the speculative perils inherent in such issues.

6. Require a written memo from customers' brokers citing the basis for recommending all low-priced issues, especially those trading in the OTC market.

7. Deny margin accommodation on stocks selling below $5.

8. Make unavailable, or provide reluctantly, statistical data on these mini-stocks.

All or many of these steps have been taken by firms not as a deliberate disservice to clients but because their research departments are simply not equipped to provide accurate current information about issues not regularly followed; because low-priced issues are a nuisance, since they require just as much paperwork as higher-priced, more profitable issues, and requests for quotes on mini-stocks tie up traders' phones during busy markets; and because firms prefer, where possible, to limit their recommendations and executions to seasoned securities with broad trading markets and extensive research data available, rather than in low prices and highly volatile securities.

Such firms are also concerned that their newer brokers may not be properly equipped by knowledge or training to counsel clients in the purchase or sale of risky lower-priced issues with thin markets; and in following the policy "know your investor," they may decide that penny stocks have no place in conservative portfolios. Finally, they may be concerned about a possible lawsuit if a customer buys a low-priced stock that "goes sour" and then blames the firm for "putting him into it."

Stock exchanges, too, have exercised surveillance over low-priced shares, especially if there appeared evidence of manipulation. To dampen speculative ardor, the AMEX, in 1968, asked four companies either to reverse split their shares (bringing them into a higher-priced trading range) or face delisting. They were delisted!

We have stressed the current plight of the low-priced or basement-level stocks because we think Wall Street errs in discouraging trading in this sector. Most new young companies start out with low-priced shares. Making venture capital available to finance or expand smaller enterprises is an essential function of capitalism. Denying market access to these mini-stocks may prevent thousands of investors, well aware of the risks involved, from making killings or even fortunes on shares that start out at low prices.

Look at the results of early investment in some originally low-priced items. You could have bought 100 shares of Occidental Petroleum at 20 cents a share in 1956. That $20 investment grew to over $13,000 by June 1968. A hundred shares of Monogram Industries bought at 1½ in 1965 grew to $5700 in market value in 1968. Between 1962 and 1968, a 100-share lot of Ogden Corp. grew from $425 to over $5200. Control Data sold at $2 in 1958 and as high as $156 in 1968. In the 1920s, Tabulating and Recording Co., a predecessor of IBM, sold at $4 a share! There are hundreds of other examples of stock like these, bought for peanuts by individuals willing to take a chance, that made killings or built fortunes.

It really didn't take a genius in the 1950s to imagine that Xerox, with its labor-saving automatic copying machine, would be a big success. Early perception of the virtues of adhesive and masking tapes might have made a fortune for you in 3M stock. Tropicana, transporting juice rather than whole oranges to your breakfast table, obviously had a winning idea. H & R Block found a major need and filled it.

Look around today for a young company with a new product or service—a minicomputer, a patented medical or surgical instrument, a new process converting wastes into fuel, a new proprietary medicine, or a style or fabric that could replace denim. Look at Lotus Corp., for example—a software company whose shares doubled the offering price within a month in early 1984. The opportunities are always there! Plan to lodge a small percentage of your investment funds in bold venturesome stocks. Spread your dollars over four or five and you're likely to get at least one good performer among them.

In looking about for gainful mini-stocks, here is some of the information you should get:

1. Where the company is located and how long it has been in business.
2. Something about the kind of business it's in and its products, services, patents, processes; its customers and markets.
3. Latest twelve months' earning statement and balance sheet.
4. Names of principal officers and some opinions as to their management capability.

5. Market range of stock in the past two years, and some indications of trading volume.
6. Current economic factors that might favor (or disfavor) company operations.
7. Does management own a substantial amount of stock (20 percent or more)?
8. Any special feature of the company: a patent, tax-loss carry forward, valuable realty, forest or mineral resources, etc.
9. Reasonable estimate of net profits in the next twelve months.

Of course this list is not a complete one, but it provides guidelines for data to help you reach an investment decision.

In current security markets there are probably over 40,000 stock issues traded, or at least quoted, each week. Of these, about 7500 are active—quoted daily on the various exchanges and in the OTC market.

In this market sector you can find shares of small, young, and growing companies possibly en route to impressive stature and profitability.

Indeed, for the bold, bankruptcies in many fields are worth exploring. In the reorganizations that follow, some dismally low-priced shares can rack up exciting percentage gains. Wall Street seems to have a unique capability to "overreact" both to bad and good news!

The message of this chapter is simple. You should not neglect consideration of a security for speculative purposes merely because a big brokerage firm does not recommend it or even disfavors it. Opportunities in low-priced shares are found in almost every industry or market sector. You can purchase such stocks from discount houses.

Your low-priced stock shopping list can include new

issues, warrants, mining shares, spinoffs, shares issued in reorganization and companies on their way up, as well as those steeped in misery, misfortune, or mismanagement. If you have courage, patience, and common sense, and get the information you need to make a logical market decision, then you may add zest to your life and enhance your net worth. But one last word: you must diversify. A low-priced stock may do one of two things: go up or blow up!

Suggested Lazarus Profit Action Possibilities

Company	Ticker Symbol	Price (as of March 23, 1984)
American Capital	ACC	7¼
Derose Industries	DRI	7⅛
Diodes	DIO	6⅜
Ero Industries	ERO	8⅞
Genetic Systems	GSY	6¼
Hoffman Industries	HOF	5½
Howell Industries	HOW	7⅜
Intercole	IC	6⅞
Jetronic	JET	5
Kinark	KIN	4⅞
MidAmerica Industries	MAM	9½
Ozark Airline	OZK	8¼
Pittsburgh & West Virginia Railroad	PW	6⅝
Sanmark-Stardust	SMK	5⅝
Sargent Industries	SGT	6¾
Seligman & Associates	SLG	3¾
Sterling Extruder	SLX	7⅜
Three-D Department	TDD-B	7¾
United Foods	UFD-B	3
Verit Industries	VER	5⅛

14

The Wonderful World
of Warrants

Brokers and investors have ever been on the alert for speculative vehicles that provide unusual leverage and opportunity for high-percentage gains with small capital outlays. The common stock warrant has for years provided such a vehicle. It is the ancestor of all the options, offered these days in such great profusion.

The warrant is the will-o'-the-wisp of finance. It has no claim on assets, nor any share in earnings, assets or dividends. It has no rights in the sale or liquidation of corporate assets; no book or par value and no voting rights. Yet it is one of the most popular low-priced speculations and has made killings and even fortunes for shrewd and agile traders.

A warrant is a security issued by a corporation giving the holder the right to purchase one or more shares (or fractions

148

of shares) of common stock in that company at a stated price and for a limited and specified period of time. Warrants are registered and negotiable. When issued in volume, they enjoy an active trading market. A few warrants are listed on the NYSE, a couple of dozen on the AMEX, and hundreds trade over-the-counter. Warrants are volatile and may range in price from pennies to $50 or more.

A spectacular example was the warrant of Charter Company in 1979. This warrant (to purchase one share of Charter at $10) soared on the NYSE from 1⅜ to a high of 45¼. A modest investment of $137.50 in 100 warrants zoomed, in less than a year, to $4,575—a gain of over 3300 percent!

The vital information about a warrant is the purchasing price of the related stock, and the expiration date. For example, the Chrysler warrant (a most popular one) represents the right to buy one share at $13 until June 1, 1985. After June 1, 1985 the warrant becomes worthless. U.S. Air, Inc. warrants call for the purchase of 1.04 shares of common at $17.31 until April 1, 1987. As this was written, the common sold at 28 and the warrant at 15.

There are a few "perpetual" warrants that have no expiration dates. Outstanding examples are Tri-Continental, Atlas Corp., and Allegheny Corp. The Allegheny warrants give the holders the right to buy one share at 3¾ without time limit.

Airlines, oil companies, and casinos have traditionally used warrants in financing, but today warrants are regularly used in new offerings of industrial and technology companies.

Warrants originate in a variety of ways:

1. In a corporate reorganization when they may be issued to troubled security holders in exchange for old stock or bonds in a bankruptcy proceeding.

2. As a sweetener to bonds in a public offering: a $1000 bond with twenty detachable warrants for example. (In many cases a bond may be offered at $1000—its face value—in lieu of cash, when the warrants are exercised.)
3. In a package of new securities: two shares of common and one warrant for a "unit" price.
4. In a merger offer, as an additional inducement to a "selling out" shareholder.

When you read the financial pages you will frequently see new offerings of debentures with warrants and packaged underwritings of stocks and warrants. Get a prospectus on the new offering. The new warrant coming on the market may develop into a big winner! Watch when the "after market" in the warrant begins. Warrants generally run from one to five years.

Try to buy warrants in the early phases of bull markets or in a depressed industry with "turnaround" prospects. Buy early, and prefer large issues with active trading markets.

Here are some helpful guidelines:

1. Buy long-term warrants—so they don't expire before the stock can move up.
2. Don't overlook the expiration date and forfeit your money.
3. Buy low—preferably below $5. A good rule is never to pay for the warrant more than one-third of the selling price of the related common stock.
4. Buy before the warrant has real value. (When General Tire common sold at 50 in 1956 there was a warrant to buy the stock at 60. The warrant was then quoted at 7. In 1958 GT stock soared to 275 and the warrant fetched 215!)
5. Select companies with dynamic upside potential; computers, communication, high-tech, service companies, etc.

When to sell? In general, look for a 200 percent gain and sell "when the clamor of the bulls is loudest." Don't exercise the warrant. Sell it and buy another promising one! You have to glean plump gains because the warrant provides no interest or dividend income.

To guide you into profit situations we submit below a number of Dowbeater warrant selections.

Name of Stock	Exercise Price & Expiration Date	Price of Stock	Price of Warrant
Golden Nugget	Purchase one common share at 18 until July, 1988	11⅝	4¼
Horn & Hardart	Purchase one common share at 20⅝ until December, 1987	18⅛	8
Collins Foods International	Purchase one common share at 27¼ until December, 1988	15¾	3⅞
Pier 1 Imports	Purchase one common share at 22 until July, 1988	14⅞	4½
Beker	Purchase one common share at 10 until July, 1988	11¼	4⅛
General Tire	Purchase one common share at 40 until March, 1988	32⅞	5¼
Tyler Corporation	Purchase one common share at 34 until November, 1987	26⅛	5⅛
MGM	Purchase one common share at 20 until April, 1988	15¼	4⅜
American General	Purchase one common share at 24¼ until January, 1989	21⅞	6¾

The universe of warrants is broad and there are hundreds of issues from which to choose. Consider the list we provide and get a new list of offerings from your broker. Watch the markets in the papers. You may want to subscribe to certain investment services specializing in warrants. Even a tired warrant—like First Pennsylvania—might come "into the money."

You may wish to devote a percentage of your West Pool portfolio to warrants. If you select well and time your purchases, you should prosper. We much prefer warrants to options which, 70 percent of the time, "drop dead" unexercised! They run for too short a period of time.

06

The Billion-Share
Short Squeeze

Among the elements in the market renaissance we envision is the increased acceptance of all types of leverage. Leverage is best described as the use of other people's money to generate larger earnings or gains for your money. Perhaps the most common example of leverage is the real estate mortgage. You may buy a $100,000 house, putting up $50,000 of your own money and borrowing $50,000 on a mortgage. Each dollar of yours then does the work of two dollars. Should you sell the house for $120,000, the $20,000 gain would represent a 40 percent return on your $50,000, but it would represent only a 20 percent return had you put up the entire $100,000 to buy the house yourself originally.

When you buy stock on margin you enjoy a leverage, presently that of 2 to 1 with a 50 percent margin requirement, whereby you supply 50 percent of the cost of your investment and the broker lends you the other 50 percent at interest. (In 1929, with only a 10 percent requirement, the leverage ratio was 10 to 1!)

Also, the capitalization of companies creates leverage for stockholders. If a company, for example, has $3 million in debt (other people's money) and $1 million in outstanding common stock, the leverage for shareholders is 3 to 1.

Options

The most popular high-leverage market vehicle today is the *call option*, introduced in 1973. It was first traded on the Chicago Board Options Exchange (CBOE). It is the first cousin of the warrant.

The call option differs from other security types in that it (1) is not issued as a certificate or bond of any corporation; (2) has no participation in the sale, liquidation, or distribution of any corporate assets; (3) never pays a dividend or interest; (4) has no voting rights; (5) is not limited to any specific number of units outstanding; (6) expires within a short period—generally nine months; (7) limits possible loss to the price paid for the option. These options are now available on about 300 different stocks and are traded on the Chicago Board of Trade and on the American, Philadelphia, Midwest, and Pacific Stock Exchanges.

The call option gives its owner the right to buy 100 shares of a particular stock, actively traded on an exchange, at a specific price and for a limited period of time. The purchase price (called the *striking price*) may be the current quotation, or several points higher. The stock is called the *underlying security*; the party originating the option is the *option writer*; the party who pays the money is the *option buyer*; and the price he pays is called the *premium*.

The call is usually originated by the outright owner of a given stock. Suppose Mr. Rich owns 100 shares of General Electric paying $2.60 a share in dividend. Mr. Rich would like to increase his income so he sells, on January 2, 1985, a nine-months call option at $50 on his 100 shares to gain $500 (less a $25 commission). The option buyer is willing to pay $500 because he believes that General Electric will advance 30 points within 9 months to $80. If it does, the profit on the $500 option will be $2500 (on 100 shares from $50 to $60). Thus by investing only $500, the option buyer stands to make almost the same profit as does the outright holder of 100 shares, but with only a tenth of the capital at risk.

The merit of a call option is that it enables the owner to participate in the price increase of the named stock with far less money invested than if he bought the stock outright. In the case of Bally, a $100 call can make the same capital gain realized by the owner of 100 shares of stock, but using a $100 investment instead of $2000. However, if the stock goes down below the option price and remains there, the entire $500 would be lost. In other words, the subject stock must go up for you to win.

In bear markets, most call options will lose money, and therefore the risks must be carefully weighed. The option speculation approach we recommend is that of the East-West Pool technique, in which you speculate only with the interest earned from the principal of your conservative capital base pool. The limitation of time is the principle hazard in option speculation. The option buyer can, however, sell his holding for whatever it would bring any time during the allotted period.

Some options (like warrants) have been amazingly profitable. Gulf Oil options on the stock at 45 could have been bought in early 1984 at $4 and as high as $30 apiece in a matter of weeks.

Most options are sold by stockholders. Some daring souls, however, sell what are called "naked" options—that is, they don't own the stock but merely are willing to bet it will not go up! If a person sells a naked option his broker will insist that he lodge sufficient money or securities with the firm to assure fulfillment of the option contract. Imagine these naked option writers in a runaway bull market—they must buy the stock quickly, possibly at a substantial loss, to cover their position. Sometimes option stocks will leap higher in a single day than the entire premium a naked option writer receives, causing instant panic. Therefore, naked option writing is one of the riskiest market operations for an investor.

Options can provide a swift leveraged "ride." They work best in bull markets when popular stocks are rising dramatically. In the past, such "swingers" as Polaroid, Bally Manufacturing, and Texas Instruments have rewarded option owners well in confident markets. Speculation in this area has become a significant source of income to brokerage firms and has notably expanded trading volume in popular issues. More important, options in the coming boom represent a powerful catalyst to explosive upside price movements.

The exponential growth in the options market has now created a sleeping giant, since a major portion of the shares represented by options are naked (uncovered), the option market has created the greatest "short position" in stock market history! As hundreds of options series, particularly naked options, are written and traded, thousands of individuals may be driven into the share market to cover their positions.

The forces that motivate modern economic man are spotlighted in the option market. Here, overnight riches (and overnight financial disasters) await avid speculators.

The Short Squeeze

Option volume is soaring into new all-time highs. In fact, the options traffic has grown 5000 percent since its inception eleven years ago, and on many days the volume of shares represented by options trading exceeds the volume on the New York Stock Exchange. If option volume continues to grow at such a pace, there will be a greater tendency for the stock market to move up with vigor, due to option short squeezes.

A small ripple in the stock market is like a tidal wave to many uncovered option writers who are trying to capitalize on short-term price movements. In an uptrending market the decisions made by these option speculators will surely stimulate major covering or hedging in the equity market.

Naked option writers (now estimated by the Chicago Board of Trade to be an average of 26 percent of all option writers) will scramble to buy stock. As one set of naked option writers covers, there will be a newer group of naked option writers who think the market is too high. With every wave of new highs, the new option shorts will scramble to cover. We will find that these short squeezes will occur sporadically, marked by sudden price moves along with record high volume on the New York Exchange. In fact, this volume expansion has become characteristic in the past few years.

As shown on Chart 9, the price explosion in Resorts International and Bally Mfg. illustrates what can happen as stock prices reach all-time highs. Once an all-time high is hit, the short positions—or, in the case of Bally Mfg., the naked option writers—rush to cover and buy the shares they do not have. Since all of these positions are put to the test within a few days, it is no wonder prices explode.

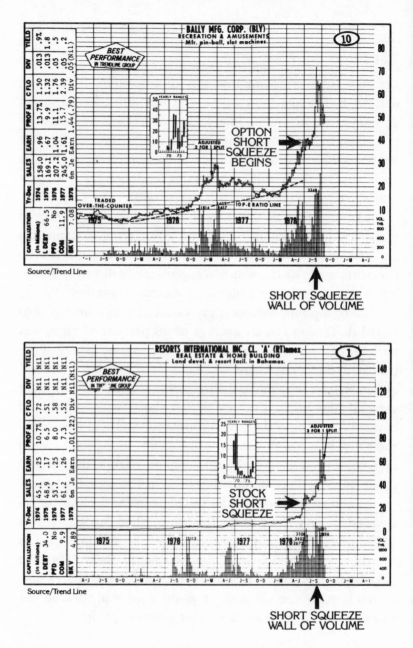

Chart 9   (*Courtesy Trendline, 345 Hudson St., N.Y. 10014*)

Repeatedly the naked option writers will be put to the squeeze, and the covered writers forced into holding long positions. As prices move up and options across the board go "in the money," all positions will have to be covered or at least hedged. (Every call option written is, in effect, a short sale.)

We are moving into a period when short squeeze action may not be limited to a particular stock or group of stocks, but emerge as an across-the-board phenomenon. As prices reach all-time highs, each short position becomes a loser, while every long position ever taken becomes a winner. This creates a squeeze on the shorts all at once. The result will be a dynamic surge in prices because more than a billion shares have been eliminated from the market's floating supply, due to the option market. The trigger point was hit when the Dow exceeded its past high of 1070. The developing panic to cover could cause a rash of equity buying, sending the prices of stocks spiraling upwards in the years ahead.

Sensational volume will then create front-page news!

After years of sideways motion, and of dull, inactive markets—after years of eroding stock prices—America will explode in the 1980s from its longest reconsolidation in modern history (as identified by the Dow). This will create a confident attitude, ushering in a new boom on Wall Street and the emergence of a new generation of investors. All of a sudden the iceberg of pessimism will melt as the Dow sizzles to new all-time highs.

In the 1980s million of investors will strive to be Dow-beaters, to outperform the averages, to outsmart the crowd. If history repeats itself the Dow will chart a pathway to unrivaled prosperity for the shrewd, the thrifty, the informed, and the patient. The future is in your hands. . . .

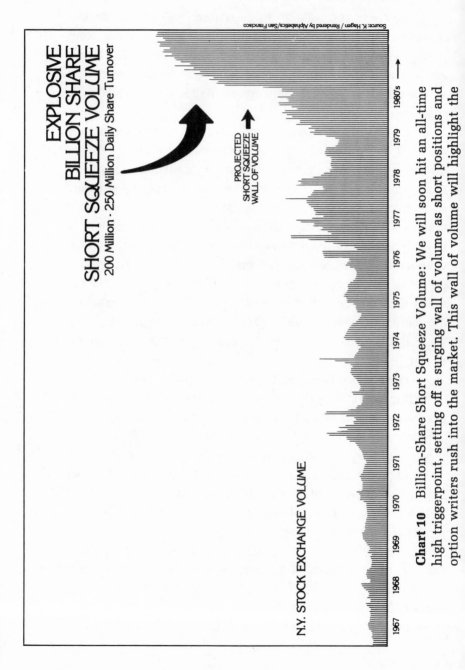

Chart 10 Billion-Share Short Squeeze Volume: We will soon hit an all-time high triggerpoint, setting off a surging wall of volume as short positions and option writers rush into the market. This wall of volume will highlight the

Glossary

ACCRUED INTEREST   The interest on a bond, note, or debenture which has been earned since the last interest payment thereon.

AMERICAN STOCK EXCHANGE   Sometimes called "the Curb," the second major securities exchange in New York.

AMEX   Abbreviation for above.

AMORTIZATION   The "writing off" of an asset over a period of time, usually at a certain annual percentage.

ANALYST   A professional evaluator of securities and economic trends.

ANNUAL REPORT   The official statement of assets, liabilities, earnings, and net worth and progress (if any), of a corporation, covering a fiscal or calendar year.

ARBITRAGE   Taking advantage of existing price differentials by simultaneous buying and selling (usually in different markets) of identical or intrinsically equivalent assets (currencies, commodities, or securities).

161

ASSETS Anything a corporation owns or is owed.

AVERAGES The various barometers of stock price trends. Best known are the Dow Jones Industrial Average, made up of thirty major stocks; the *New York Times* Average of fifty stocks; Standard & Poor's Average of four hundred twenty-five industrial stocks; NYSE Common Stock Index, a composite of all "listed" common stocks.

BALANCE SHEET A financial statement revealing the assets, liabilities, capital, and net worth of a company on a specific date.

BANKRUPTCY Where a corporation's liabilities exceed its assets and it is unable to meet its current obligations. There are two kinds: Chapter 11, Voluntary—where an accommodation with creditors may be worked out, and Chapter 10, Involuntary—where assets under court order are placed in the hands of a referee for disposition to satisfy creditors (usually but not always).

BEAR A person who thinks stocks are going down, and who may sell stock "short" to back up his opinions.

BEAR MARKET A declining one.

BID-AND-ASKED A quotation of the best price which will be paid, and the lowest-priced offering of a security at a given moment.

BIG BOARD The New York Stock Exchange.

BLUE CHIP The common stock of a major company, with a long record of earnings and dividends.

BLUE SKY LAWS Laws in many states protecting investors against being sold a slice of "the blue sky," i.e., a fraudulent, mythical, or misrepresented security.

BOARD ROOM Sitting room for stock traders in a broker's office.

BOILER ROOM A place where second-rate or worthless securities are sold to the gullible—usually over the phone.

BOND The long-term obligation of a corporation to repay a given sum (usually in $1,000 denominations) on a given date, with a specified rate of interest to be paid at regular intervals until then. Bonds can be debentures (unsecured), or protected by collateral, lien, or mortgage on corporate property.

BOND PRICES Quotations, given as percentages of par value.

BOOK VALUE   All the assets of a company, less all liabilities and the par value of preferred stocks (if any) divided by the number of common shares outstanding.

BROKER   A financial agent associated with a member of a stock exchange or a broker/dealer firm, who executes orders in securities or commodities on a commission basis.

BULL   A person believing that the market will rise, and aiming to profit if it does.

CALL OPTION   A contract to buy 100 shares of a stock at a specified price, for a limited period of time.

CALLABLE   A bond or preferred stock that may be redeemed and retired under certain conditions and at a specified price.

CAPITAL ASSETS   The fixed assets of a company, a factory, office building, plant, warehouse, trucks, etc.

CAPITAL GAIN OR LOSS   Profit or loss realized when a security (or other asset) is sold.

CAPITAL STOCK   The shares which represent the ownership of, or equity in, a company.

CAPITALIZATION   The entire amount of all securities (debt and equity) issued by a corporation.

CASH FLOW   The net income of a company (for a given period) to which are added depletion, depreciation, amortization charges, and nonrecurring charges to reserves; frequently stated "per share."

CATS AND DOGS   Low-priced stocks of dubious worth.

CBOE   Chicago Board Option Exchange.

CERTIFICATES OF DEPOSIT (CDS)   Short interest-bearing obligations of banking institutions, secured by deposits.

CHARTS   Statistical data about prices, volume, and trends in different stocks, portrayed graphically, hopefully to indicate the future direction of prices.

COLLATERAL   Property, most frequently securities, pledged to secure interest and repayment of a loan.

COMMERCIAL PAPER   The short-term notes or obligations of substantial corporations, maturing customarily within 12 months' time.

COMMISSION   The fee charged by a broker to execute an order to buy or sell.

COMMON STOCKS The ownership or equity interest in a corporation, with a claim on assets or earnings, coming after preferred stocks, notes, bonds, or other indebtedness.

CONGLOMERATE A company which has accumulated as subsidiaries a group of companies in many different and unrelated lines of business.

CONTROL The group owning enough stock (customarily 51 percent or more), or influencing enough stockholders, to direct the affairs of a corporation.

CONVERTIBLE A bond or preferred stock, which may, under certain conditions, be exchanged for common stock, usually in the same company.

CORPORATION A legally organized intangible organization operating (usually) under a state charter with (1) unlimited life, (2) limited liability, and (3) transferable certificates representing shares of ownership.

COUPON BOND One which pays interest semi-annually by means of detachable coupons which can be cashed when due.

CUMULATIVE PREFERRED A stock which may pay at a later date any omitted regular dividends, and on which all past due dividends must be paid before the common stock can receive any distribution.

CURRENT ASSETS Assets in cash, receivables, short-term securities, and items collectible and convertible into cash within a year.

CURRENT LIABILITIES What a company owes that must be paid within a year.

CUSTOMER'S MAN A representative of a stock exchange firm.

CUT A MELON To declare a substantial extra dividend, usually in stock.

CYCLICAL STOCKS Those whose earnings tend to fluctuate with the business cycle.

DEBENTURE A kind of bond, unsecured by lien or mortgage on any specific property.

DELISTED When a security is removed from trading on a stock exchange, and reverts to the OTC market.

DEPLETION A bookkeeping charge against earnings to mark the lower remaining value of a natural resource holding (coal, oil, minerals, timber) after some part of it has been removed, extracted, or exhausted.

DEPRECIATION A bookkeeping charge against earnings to write down the cost of an asset over its useful life.

DIRECTOR A person elected by company shareholders to be a member of its Board of Directors and a maker of corporate policies and decisions.

DIVERSIFICATION The spreading of investments among many different securities and industries.

DIVIDEND A payment authorized by a Board of Directors, either in cash or in stock, pro rata among shareholders. Usually a distribution made from current or past profits.

DOLLAR COST AVERAGING Applying a level sum of money each year, say $1000, to the purchase of as many shares of a stock as those dollars will buy at then-prevailing prices.

DOW THEORY An attempt to project market trends on the basis of the correlated past market action of 30 industrial and 20 transportation stocks.

ECONOMIST A social scientist, often in error but seldom in doubt.

EQUITY The interest in a company represented by ownership of either (or both) its common or preferred stock.

EX DIVIDEND (X) Indicates that the stock, if bought, does not carry with it the dividend most recently declared.

EXTRA Any declaration in stock or cash above regular or customary dividend distribution.

FEDERAL RESERVE BOARD The quasi-government agency controlling the supply and price of money and regulating installment credit and margin loans.

FISCAL YEAR The official accounting year of a corporation (usually), when it does not coincide with the calendar year.

FIXED CHARGES Fixed expenses of a corporation which must be paid whether earned or not—most commonly interest charges or rentals.

FLOOR The trading area on a stock exchange.

FUNDAMENTAL ANALYSIS Evaluation of a stock on the basis of its earnings, assets, profit margins, dividends, and investment stature.

FUNDED DEBT Long-term interest-bearing obligations of a company, most commonly bonds and debentures.

GILT-EDGED A high-grade bond, so called because it referred originally to issues payable (before 1933) in dollars convertible into gold.

GOING PUBLIC The public offering of a company's securities for the first time.

GROWTH STOCK A company whose sales, earnings, and net worth are expanding at an unusual rate.

GTC An order good until cancelled (or executed).

INSIDER A person or corporation owning 10 percent or more of the stock of a public company, who must report to SEC each month any substantial changes in holdings.

INTEREST The price paid for use or rental of money, expressed as a percentage per annum.

INVESTMENT BANKER An individual or a firm buying securities for resale to others. Also called an underwriter.

INVESTMENT COUNSEL An individual or firm paid a fee to advise and/or manage investment accounts.

INVESTMENT TRUST A company which gathers funds from individuals, and which invests these funds in a portfolio of diversified securities, professionally managed. There are "open end" trusts (called mutual funds) whose outstanding shares vary in number from day to day.

LAMB A gullible investor.

LEVERAGE Using other people's money to generate earnings or gain for you, as when large amounts of senior securities exist in a corporate capitalization, ahead of its common stock. Leverage is also created by using borrowed money to buy stocks (or a house with a mortgage).

LIABILITIES Any and all legal claims against a company.

LIEN A mortgage or other legal claim against property to secure a debt.

LIQUIDITY The capability of an investment to be converted quickly into cash. Checking and savings account deposits are highly liquid; so are CDs, and commercial paper and prime short-term securities (municipal, government, or corporate notes).

LISTED STOCK   Shares trading on any stock exchange (most commonly the New York, American, and regional stock exchanges).

LONG   Means that you own a specific security or securities, as opposed to a short position where you sell what you don't own.

MANAGEMENT   The officers of a company and the board of directors which elects them.

MANIPULATION   The illegal "rigging" of stock prices by artificial stimulation, sometimes involving the spread of incorrect information.

MARGIN   The sum of money or value of securities deposited with a broker to purchase securities. Margin requirements (currently 50 percent of the cost of securities purchased) are determined at intervals by the Federal Reserve Board. Margin purchase is designed to enable a person to buy more securities than his own resources would permit.

MARGIN CALL   A broker's request to put up more money or collateral to protect security holdings that have declined, and that were purchased in part on borrowed money.

MARKET ORDER   An order to buy or sell at the best obtainable price then prevailing.

MERGER   When two or more companies are joined together.

MUNICIPALS   A generic germ for bonds issued by counties, cities, states, districts, or public authorities, usually with the interest payments exempt from federal taxation.

MUTUAL FUND   *See:* Investment Trust.

NEW ISSUE   The first public offering of a bond or stock.

NEW YORK STOCK EXCHANGE   The world's leading auction market for securities.

NYSE   Abbreviation for above.

ODD LOT   A small amount of stock, customarily less than 100 shares.

OPEN END FUND   A mutual fund or investment trust wherein shares are bought or sold only by the trust, with the amount of publicly held shares constantly changing as new shares are bought and old shares redeemed.

OVER-THE-COUNTER   The largest, and a nationwide, telephone

and electronic market for those securities not regularly traded on any exchange.

OTC   Abbreviation for above.

PAPER PROFIT   Unrealized indicated gain on a security still held.

PAR VALUE   .Face or nominal value of a security.

PENNY SHARES   Customarily those selling at $1.00 or less.

PERFORMANCE STOCK   One that gains spectacularly in price (or is expected to!).

PER SHARE NET   Total net earnings of a company after taxes, for a given period, divided by the number of common shares outstanding.

POINT   A point is $1.00 on stocks or $10 on a bond.

PORTFOLIO   The total security holdings of an individual or institution.

PREFERRED STOCK   A stock having a claim on a company's earnings or assets, ahead of its common stock, and usually entitled to dividends at a fixed rate.

PREMIUM   The amount by which a bond or preferred stock sells above its face amount, or a new issue sells above its offering price.

PRICE/EARNINGS RATIO   The current price of a stock, divided by the per-share net earnings of the issuing company, for the most recently reported twelve-month period. (Also called "P/E Multiple.")

PRIME RATE   The interest rate charged by banks to their best customers on unsecured loans.

PRINCIPAL   A person or firm who buys and sells for his own account.

PROSPECTUS   A summary of all the pertinent history, facts, and figures about a company and the people who run it, prior to a new securities offering. By law, a prospectus must be presented to a possible buyer in advance of any purchase.

PROXY   Designation, by a stockholder, of someone else to represent him at a stockholder's meeting.

PUTS AND CALLS   Options to buy (a call) or to sell (a put) a certain number of shares of a stock at fixed prices for limited periods of time.

QUOTATION The bid-and-asked price of a security.

RED HERRING An early prospectus draft, omitting the offering price of the issue.

REGISTERED REPRESENTATIVE A person approved by the Stock Exchange to handle orders for the purchase or sale of securities for clients. Also called an Account Executive and, formerly, a Customer's Man or Customer's Broker.

REFINANCING The issuance of new securities to refund outstanding ones or to retire or extend a debt.

REGISTRATION The filing of information about a forthcoming security offering with the Securities and Exchange Commission (national regulatory body) preliminary to preparation and printing of a prospectus.

RIGHTS The privilege, given to a shareholder, to buy additional stock in a company for a limited time and at a special price.

SEC The Securities and Exchange Commission, a federal organization for the regulation of the securities industry.

SECONDARY DISTRIBUTION Offering of securities, previously issued, in which the company receives no share of the proceeds.

SENIOR SECURITIES Bonds, notes, and preferred stocks ranking ahead of common stock.

SHORT SALE Selling stock sold "short" (that is, not owned) with a view to buying it back later at a lower price; the stock is borrowed for delivery meanwhile (usually from a broker).

SHORT-TERM PAPER Notes due within a year; commercial paper and certificates of deposit.

SINKING FUND Money reserved by a corporation to buy in, and redeem, its own senior securities.

SPECIALIST A floor member of an exchange designated to maintain an orderly market in specified securities and to act as a broker's broker.

SPECULATION The employment of funds and assumption of risks primarily to create capital gains.

SPIN-OFFS The delivery by a parent company to its stockholders of shares in another corporation.

SPLIT Increasing the outstanding number of shares in a company by division of the existing ones.

STOCK DIVIDEND A dividend paid not in cash but in securities.

STOP ORDER   An instruction to sell when and if a security reaches a certain price.

STREET NAME   Stock held in the name of a broker or nominee instead of the legal owner.

SWEETENER   A convertible privilege or a warrant attached to a senior security to make the issue more attractive and to thus reduce its interest or dividend rate.

SYNDICATE   A group of security firms cooperating with the underwriting firm in the distribution of a security issue.

TAX EXEMPT BOND   One with its interest payments exempt from federal income taxation.

TECHNICAL ANALYSIS   Evaluation of stocks on the basis of their recent market performance, volume, and price trends.

THIN MARKET   One in which there are few bids and offerings and (often) wide "spreads" between them.

TICKER   The electric device which immediately reports and transmits on tape prices and volumes of security transactions.

TIPS   Confidential urgings to buy certain securities, supposed to be based on information "from the horse's mouth."

TRADING POST   U-shaped booths on the floor of the NYSE, each one assigned to trade about 75 different stocks.

TRADING SYMBOLS   The abbreviations containing no more than three letters for listed stocks; sometimes four for OTC issues.

TRANSFER   The official recording of charge in ownership of a security, performed by a transfer agent.

TREASURY BILLS   Short-term (usually no longer than six months) interest-bearing obligations of the U.S. government.

TREASURY STOCK   Stock formerly outstanding but repurchased by the company.

UNLISTED   (*See* Over-the-Counter) Name given to those securities not listed on any exchange but traded over-the-counter.

UTILITIES   A broad classification of corporate monopolies, including gas, electric, telephone, and water companies.

WARRANT   A certificate authorizing its owner to buy a share, shares (or fractions) of common stock of a company at a specific price and during a specified time period.

WHEN ISSUED A security trading regularly, but not available for actual delivery until some future date.

WIRE HOUSE A NYSE member firm connected with its branch offices or correspondents by direct telephone or teletype circuits.

YIELD The return on investment in a given security at its current price, expressed as a percentage. To determine the yield on a stock, divide the present indicated annual dividend by the market price of a single share.

Index